Unlocked

To my family and friends, with love
To my clients, with affection and gratitude

Unlocked

Online Therapy Stories

Anastasia Piatakhina Giré

First published in 2022 by Confer Books, an imprint of Confer Ltd
www.confer.uk.com

Registered office:
Brody House, Strype Street, London E1 7LQ

1 3 5 7 9 10 8 6 4 2

British Library Cataloguing in Publication Data
A catalogue record for this book is available from the British Library.

ISBN: 978-1-913494-42-1 (paperback)
ISBN: 978-1-913494-43-8 (ebook)

Typeset by Bespoke Publishing Ltd.
Printed in the UK by Ashford Colour Press.

CONTENTS

PROLOGUE   vii

I   **Laila,** *Riyadh, Saudi Arabia*   **1**

II   **Jane,** *London, UK*   **17**

III   **Alan,** *Manhattan, New York*   **35**

IV   **Anna,** *Venice, Italy*   **55**

V   **JP,** *Brussels, Belgium*   **75**

VI   **Alice,** *London, UK*   **101**

VII   **Claudio,** *Rome, Italy*   **129**

VIII **Elena,** *New Jersey*   **159**

IX   **Claire,** *Paris, France*   **189**

X   **Philip,** *Northumberland, UK*   **229**

PROLOGUE

When the pandemic hit the world, I had already been seeing my therapy clients online (via video-conferencing) for a decade. Unlike most other people, my work flow and my daily routine were hardly impacted. My colleagues who had been practising in person in a therapy room had to switch to online overnight. My clients and I were already used to meeting through the lens of our webcams, and seeing each other's faces on the screen. It allowed our work to be uninterrupted.

That very dramatic moment was a rare situation in which all of us – therapists and clients – were dealing with the same major crisis, in a very similar context, becoming fellow travellers facing the same storm.

All therapeutic work described in this book happens online. Not long ago therapists met remote work with suspiciousness, feeling that the use of technology can reduce therapy to something 'less'. These stories show the contrary, demonstrating how a curious and skilled online therapist can make the most of the unexpected gifts that 'screen' therapy offers – be it the intrusion of a pet, a parent breaking into the session or a client taking her therapist for a trip outside. This book takes therapeutic conversations out of the confinement of a physical therapy room, breathing a new energy and new possibilities into the therapeutic process. Therapeutic conversations that happen through the screen have a surprising close-up quality and foster a different kind of intimacy and intensity.

My remote therapy work during the pandemic provided inspiring and humbling lessons. It brought me back to the Stoic philosophers who, as timely as ever, teach us that the obstacles that we encounter are actually fuel. 'The impediment to action advances action. What stands in the way becomes the way', wrote Marcus Aurelius. Any obstacle has a paradoxical ability to also be the vehicle by which we surmount the obstacle. Every hour spent with my online clients during these challenging times also reminded me about the resilience and the creative potential of human nature.

Crisis has a powerful capacity not only to reveal us as people, but also to make apparent some previously hidden knowledge about our life 'before'. This is when therapy is most efficient, exploiting this revealing potential, turning life obstacles into fuel that allows impressive break-throughs.

There is no need to preach the power of therapy in facilitating individual change; the power of *online* therapy, which used to be widely questioned, is probably more peculiar. During the pandemic, the limits of remote therapy have been stretched and it has shown its full potential – its power to get us out of a locked room. A simple computer screen turns into a window towards the other. Even with an unstable internet connection (a widespread concern about online therapy), technology makes a strong human connection possible, which is the most powerful ingredient of any therapeutic success.

Each story in this book is a therapeutic investigation into one particular client's life crisis and its underlying psychological issue. The therapeutic dialogue between the therapist and her client is charged in suspense. It leads us, not unlike a good whodunit, towards a resolution that will inspire the reader to re-think the potential for change that his or her own personal crisis may offer.

It also reveals part of the therapist's own story that informs her work. Throughout the ten case studies, the reader gathers different sides of the therapist's personality and background, ending up with a sense of who she is. This echoes what happens in therapy – without the therapist self-disclosing much, the client will get to know her in time.

There is certainly no perfect solution to the problem of writing about therapy patients, and each therapist-turned-writer has tried in their own way to perform this balancing act – between respecting their clients' confidentiality and the need for a therapeutic story, from which other therapists and clients may learn. I have tried my best to do this as well. Inspired by real clients who I was seeing in online therapy during the pandemic, these stories are heavily fictionalised. Personal details have been modified and disguised, in order to fully protect my clients' identities. The therapist who narrates the ten stories is also fictional, although resembling me at times.

Marcus Aurelius (2002). *Meditations: A New Translation,* by Gregory Hays. New York: Random House.

I

Laila

Riyadh, Saudi Arabia

Laila is very good at hiding. This is the first time we meet, and as her unveiled face appears on my screen, I can barely distinguish her features hidden by the thick darkness of the room.

From her initial email, I know that Laila is in her late 30s, unmarried and, as a result of these circumstances, is living in her parents' house in a very conservative Middle Eastern country. She warns me straightaway that it has been a difficult and risky decision for her to engage in therapy, especially online and with a western therapist. It is also her only option if she wants to keep it away from her family and confidential.

Privacy is an issue. Her parents' house is vast and has many rooms, but her nine siblings come and go as they wish, following the rhythms of their prayers, meals and social obligations. Some of them are married, and their young children are constantly running around the house, untamed and loud.

Connecting with Laila for our first session, I automatically become an accomplice in her rule-breaking behaviour. Starting as partners-in-crime results in an immediate intimacy and a strange sense of kinship that usually takes time to create in therapy.

"Where are you now? Is this your room?"

"Yes, it is my room, and fortunately the door is locked."

I overhear children's voices and some music resonating from the bowels of the house. By contrast, her room is very quiet and, from the little I can see of it, rather spartan.

"I told them I was having a migraine and had to lie down."

"Do you have migraines often?" She smiles sadly: "Yes, I do."

As we would realise later, this was the only excuse she had found as a child to isolate herself and get some personal space. Nevertheless, Laila's migraines' 'purpose' does not make them any less real or painful. They can last for days, and self-isolating in a dark room has become a habit that her family accepts as another bothersome part of her character, alongside the irritating stubbornness that she displays on certain occasions. The recently installed lock on her door, which has caused many heated conversations with her father, is also the welcome consequence of her 'condition'.

"I am not sure therapy can help me. Something terrible is about to happen …"

Before she can finish, we are interrupted by a strong knock on the door. Shaken by its invasive forcefulness and Laila's abrupt backing away, I do not have time to fully realise what is happening, and she is gone. My screen suddenly goes blank.

For several days, I can't stop thinking about this aborted session, worrying for Laila and wondering whether she will ever make it back to my virtual therapy room. In the meantime, Paris empties as a result of the lockdown. Bewildered Parisians watch its deserted streets from their windows or balconies. Their screens become the only way of maintaining a connection with others. The fleeting conversation with Laila is nearly forgotten when an email from her arrives. This time she is resolved to start working with me, as soon as I am free. We arrange to reconnect the following evening.

Laila

As Laila joins the video call, her face instantly fills my screen in an unexpected close-up. She is wearing a dark purple hijab neatly framing the beautifully defined features of her face. A fierce energy emanates from her. No distance or screen dampens that down.

Laila tells me that she has been postponing therapy for years, unsure of how to proceed. It started with her parents insisting that she consult a local psychiatrist, perplexed as they were by her moodiness and unwillingness to engage in any discussions about marriage plans. Laila hated it. One of her older brothers, chosen to drive her to the appointment (as she was obviously not allowed to drive), would wait for her in the corridor. She could feel his presence behind the door and his annoyance at what was just another time-consuming task for him.

***

The psychiatrist did not unveil anything (nor did Laila unveil her face in his presence). He did not seem very interested in her concerns and promptly prescribed antidepressants and a break from work. It convinced Laila not to come back to this or any other local doctor. Taking a pill would not make her problems go away. The risk of being forced to leave her job scared her.

She works as a nurse in the maternity ward of a large hospital and, strangely enough, her work has become her most cherished space in finding some privacy. There, she is valued for her skills, away from her father's constant scrutiny.

"How do you feel about talking with me, a western woman living thousands of miles away?"

"I do not know if I can trust you. But I have no choice."

I tell her that confidentiality is the very basis of therapy, but I don't know if my words are enough to reassure her.

So here we are – two women sitting in front of their computers in two opposite parts of the world – talking with each other through

3

a screen, in a language that is neither one's mother tongue. Having grown up in an autocratic state, I know too well that a foreign language can turn into a space of freedom, a boundary and a safety blanket, unavailable in one's mother tongue.

Laila has to talk in a hushed voice. Her family members are constantly passing by her room, and sometimes I clearly distinguish their voices resonating in the tiled corridors of her parents' vast house, approaching and vanishing again.

Do they speak English? Yes, a bit, but not as well as her. Laila has been passionate about learning English since her teens. She has always felt that this language offered her a space for free thinking and privacy, which she considers unattainable to her in Arabic. Her father has always scolded her for spending too much time reading in English or watching American films, but since she has had to study English for her nursing degree and, later on, to work at the international hospital, he has grudgingly conceded her this 'frivolousness'.

Since her late teens, Laila has been avidly using social media, where she now has the majority of her meaningful social connections, her 'online friends,' as she calls these virtual bonds. In this parallel world, women are able to befriend men; friends can exchange unveiled pictures of each other, discuss intimate topics and even share their religious doubts.

"Last time we spoke, you said that something terrible was about to happen. What did you mean?"

Laila shoots a quick look towards the door as if to check that nobody is there to intrude her space, but the house is silent.

"My parents received another marriage proposal for me … they know that this is maybe the last chance to get rid of me."

"Do you know this man?"

"No, but his mother is coming tomorrow to look at me."

Laila lowers her head and slips away from the camera, so that only a part of her forehead, covered by the hijab, stays visible.

The marriage hunt started when she was eighteen, and her parents' attempts to find her a suitable husband have become ever more determined and desperate. First Laila could highlight the flaws in the aspiring grooms that would make good deal-breakers: lack of a respectable career, a physical defect or, even more convincing for her parents, lack of religious fervour. As time went by, the suitors grew older, their flaws became more obvious, but her parents' desire to finally settle their insubordinate daughter also became more urgent.

This time, it is an older cousin who is already married and is now considering taking a second wife.

"I am getting too old to be a first wife … but not old enough to be left in peace." Laila's voice cracks and she is close to tears.

That evening I find it hard to join in the conversation over the now-traditional online aperitif with friends. The mundane topics around COVID symptoms, current government strategy and facemasks feel far removed from what I am still struggling with: the prospect of a forced marriage on Laila.

This is one of those times when I almost physically stumble on the limits of what I am able to offer to a client; therapy can be an empowering force but certain brute realities of existence can have a stronger adverse effect. I desperately want Laila to be free, and the intensity of my yearning is only a distant pale echo of what she is probably feeling, trying to get to sleep in her lonely room. The laughter of my friends and the jazz in the background are making Laila's isolation even more blatant in my mind.

I grew up as an only child and, at bedtime, my desolate condition would usually feel cruel. I would lie in bed for hours, fantasising about potential siblings, little doll-like brothers and sisters to dress and feed. Laila, on the contrary, has many siblings but this did not make her any less lonely; none of them understood her stubborn rebellion against the family rules or arranged marriage. I imagine her sitting on her single bed, scrolling through on her laptop her online friends' intimate messages. Would she be able to act on what we had plotted, maybe foolishly, together?

That night I dream that I am lost in a strange place – maybe an abandoned hotel or a school – unable to get out of its intricate staircases, endless corridors, and vast empty rooms. I am pacing through the rooms as a forlorn ghost, unable to find an exit or someone to ask for directions. Rescued by the morning alarm, I have to lie down for a few seconds, trying to distinguish the harrowing dream from the nightmarish reality of another lockdown day.

During the day I find myself checking emails between sessions, hoping to hear from Laila, but she keeps silent. Or is she kept silent? In my current monotonous reality, Laila's story starts to resemble a television drama with weekly episodes on my computer screen. I do not need Netflix, as my clients' real-life stories are filling the void left by the lockdown that has robbed me of many of my daily joys. Laila's distress washes me away in a powerful emotional wave that I am unable or unwilling to control; I find myself washed out on the shore of my balcony, covered with the debris of my own frustration, hurt and with a deep feeling of loss. I stand there contemplating the grey field of Parisian rooftops with hundreds of red chimneys erected in a frozen dance; birds are swirling in the still air, oblivious to the lockdown. For the first time I regret not smoking, as a cigarette would probably have been a good kick right now. My tea has become cold and tasteless. I go to the kitchen and pour myself a large glass of crisp white Burgundy.

By the time I go to bed – later with every passing day – Laila's email is waiting for me in my inbox: *"I barricaded myself in the room as planned. Did not come out when the man's mother came. I don't know what happened there. Have to go now, as my father wants to talk. Will write later."*

My heart starts racing; I know I should not be checking my emails at this time, but the lockdown seems to have altered many rules. I know that I have to do something. I go to the bathroom and wash my face with cold water. I look in the mirror and dislike what I see – an ageing woman with unkempt hair and puffy eyes. Since hairdressers shut down, my usually dark curls are showing more and more grey. I open the drawer, fetch the scissors and start cutting, methodically, until the sink is filled with hair. As I cut, I think about my husband telling me that he really prefers women with long hair; all the things I could not say no to come over me like a big wave. My own anger takes me by surprise; how can I have all this inside, after all these years of therapy, trying to heal? Then I realise that this is not just about me, but also about Laila. I am outraged and rebelling on her behalf.

***

Next time we meet online, the connection takes a while to settle, like the surface of a lake disturbed by the stone thrown by a child, and her bright face appears. She looks at me in bewilderment and I start thinking that something has gone wrong. But before I can utter a word, Laila takes her hijab off in a resolute gesture. This is the first time I see her head uncovered – she looks like a little girl, and her hair is even shorter than mine, she is almost bald. We stare at each other in amazement and the mirroring effect of our screen encounter becomes even more striking. She is the first to talk.

"I cut my hair. You did too?"

"Yes, I did."

"If my father finds out, he will be really mad."

"Do you want him to see it?"

She keeps silent for a moment, playing with her hijab, which is lying on her lap like a little dead animal.

"In a way I do, even if I am scared he may kill me."

"Kill you?"

"I mean … I don't know. I never did anything like this before."

She looks directly into the camera; in her wide-open eyes I see a mixture of excitement and defiance. Now it is my turn to feel scared.

"But does he really need to know?"

"No, maybe not yet."

With her naked head she looks so young and vulnerable that I want to protect her, to make sure she is safe. But I have to remind myself that she came to me in search of empowerment. Trusting me, she took a risk, and it is now my turn to trust her. I feel like the parent of a toddler who is climbing a jungle gym for the first time, realising that the child could fall and hurt themselves, but also has to learn this new skill in order to eventually master it.

"My father called me yesterday after he learnt I did not show up in the reception room. He was very upset."

"Is this over now or will she return?"

"Anyway not before the lockdown is over."

"Oh, good. This gives us a few weeks to figure something out."

"Yes. I do not want to marry, ever."

She stares at me with her intense dark eyes and I desperately look for words to reassure her, but I stumble as I am not certain that we can fight against her father's will, the omnipotent power over his daughter given to him by his country's tradition and law.

"Can you talk about it with your mother?"

"I tried. She keeps repeating that I have to marry and have children, otherwise I will never be happy. She does not know any other way."

"What about your older sisters?"

"They all wanted to get married. Now they think I should too."

"What about your online friends?"

"Yes, they understand. We talked about the ways out. They advise me to get ill or to lose a lot of weight. Just to gain some time."

Laila shows me her room. It looks like a prison cell, although the bare necessities for a reasonably comfortable life are there. The only objects Laila cherishes are a few books on a shelf and a television. But even those tend to attract the unwanted attention from her family – why doesn't she watch television in the common room? Why does she need all these *American* books?

The electric light is always on, even though the bright Middle East sun shines outside nearly all year around.

"We are strong on privacy here," Laila explains.

The shutters are closed all the time, to prevent neighbours getting a glimpse of the women of the house. As a result, Laila has no access to the outside world. Before the lockdown, almost her only outings consisted in commuting to her workplace in her brother's car, with tinted windows for the same reasons of privacy, making everything outside look bleak and slightly unreal. Laila recognises that often she feels like a ghost, as the familiar world turns into an uncanny copy of what reality is supposed to be. The days go by in a sort of depleted way, a succession of small familiar tasks, starting with making coffee for her father, ending with the evening prayer. Only then, as she finally locks her door behind her, taking off her hijab, does Laila feel that she is still alive.

After our session I gasp for fresh air. The balcony is not enough; I also feel a terrible itch to be moving. I put my running shoes on and venture outside after signing the compulsory *'attestation de déplacement dérogatoire'* ('self-declaration form for travel'). I feel rebellious again and, as I start running, I take my mask off my face and shove it into my pocket. The prospect of a police patrol stopping me only heightens my resolve.

The riverbanks are closed, but I ignore the warning sign as I sprint down to the calm and vast Seine. As I follow the river, very close to the edge, I can smell its slightly rotten water, finally free of pollution. The water carries a sense of calm power, vague possibility and quiet hope. But Laila lives in a desert. I have not run properly for weeks and the air soon starts hurting my lungs. I ignore the pain and keep pushing towards the Eiffel Tower, looking ghostly and slightly out of place in the middle of the empty city.

**

The next time I connect for the session with Laila, it is with a palpable sense of dread in my stomach. I realise that Laila is late, which is unusual. I open Telegram, our prearranged back-up option, only to find a message from her asking to chat here instead. Of course, we can. This is not the time for worrying about strict boundaries.

"My father found out that I'd cut my hair and confiscated my computer. He thinks that it is all because of the American films."

"How did he find out?"

"I think my mother told him. She tells him everything."

"How are you doing?"

"It does not make such a difference to me. It is just that my door is locked on the other side."

Using a chat room adds the option of staying hidden. Laila seems comfortable with this new set-up; I am less used to sudden restrictions. She is so accustomed to things being taken away from her that it does not seem to throw her out of balance.

"For how long will you be punished?"

"I don't know. It depends on his mood."

"Has it happened before?"

"Yes. When I was a teenager I spent a lot of time in here, but I actually liked it. It gave me some peace … this is when I studied English."

The language that she learnt while imprisoned has eventually become her space of freedom. Ironically, we use English for a therapy session, both being in breach of her country's expectations. As we are chatting with our respective doors locked, it feels like two teenagers secretly communicating behind their parents' backs.

"As a teen, did you have friends to talk with?"

"No. Not really. I did not have social media back then."

Laila is sounding distant. Is she typing something to her friends simultaneously?

"Can I ask you about something?"

I am glad that she asks, whatever the question may be.

"Do you think about me sometimes?"

If she only knew how much I have, she would probably feel uncomfortable.

"I do. I worry for you. And sometimes I wonder how much I am really helping you."

"You don't know how much you have been helping me."

I am regretting that this conversation is taking place by chat, but again, we have to settle for what we have. I would prefer to see her eyes, even if the screen turns eye contact into a weird imagination game. Doing with less, turning things around: these are lockdown lessons that Laila has had to master well before many of us.

***

It is the sixth week of lockdown and I am lying in bed at midnight, unable to calm down the frenetic flow of my thoughts.

All the little things that my life 'before' was made of are spinning in my mind – a coffee with a friend in the nearby café, a chat with the friendly waiter at the bistro where I stop by for lunch, a stroll to an art museum, a quick drive to the seaside for a lunch of oysters, outside under the pale Normandy sun – all things made impossible by the need to keep away from others. In the end, life's pleasures are a lot about being with or at least near others.

As I am quietly mourning all things lost, my phone buzzes, announcing a Telegram call. Before picking up, I notice that the screen displays an international number with a prefix I cannot place.

"It's Laila."

Her now familiar voice is filled with a mixture of dread and excitement; I suddenly feel completely awake, with a jolt of adrenalin rushing into my blood.

"Where are you, are you ok?"

"I am in Bangkok … at the airport. I ran away."

"Are you alone? Does your family know where you are?"

"I don't know. I am so scared … if they find me, they will kill me."

Her voice is that of a little girl; the kind of voice my daughter would have when waking up from a horrible nightmare in the middle of the night.

"How can I help you?"

"You cannot. It is too dangerous. My online friends are helping."

She keeps silent for a moment; I am waiting for her to reassure me that everything is ok, that she will be fine somehow. My heart is pounding heavily in my chest.

"Laila …? Are you there?"

"I have to go now! I just wanted to say goodbye and … thank you."

Before I am able to respond, she is gone, her voice abruptly replaced by the long beep of a dead line. As I put down the phone, I suddenly understand all that I have been missing. Everything clicks into place. Laila had been preparing her escape all along. I feel betrayed, like an object that fulfilled its purpose and can now be discarded. After a few moments the hurt gives way to anxiety: what will happen to Laila now? I pick up my phone again and start scrolling the international news. No mention of a Saudi girl on the run. Not yet.

The next time the phone comes alive in my hands, it is past midnight. Laila sounds different, she talks with a new urgency that makes me sit up in bed, alert.

"Why didn't you tell me about your plan?"

"I couldn't. It was too dangerous."

I can now hear some muffled male voices and a noise as if somebody is banging on a door.

"Where are you now? What is happening there?"

"I am in a hotel room, still at the airport. Look at the news."

Laila disconnects or maybe the call drops out.

I return to the live news page still open on my phone screen: this time Laila is there. I recognise her frail silhouette in the slightly blurred images. A short video shows her walking through a dark corridor flanked by several men in uniform – Thai police most probably. They escort her somewhere. With her black T-shirt, a red backpack and an uncovered head, Laila could easily pass for a normal teenager were it not for the policemen with watchful looks surrounding her in a tight circle. She looks vulnerable but proud.

This time I call her back; she responds in a second.

"What is your plan?"

"To ask for asylum. I am not leaving this room until I see somebody from the United Nations."

As we talk, I can hear the banging on the door and the voices getting closer again; something smashes loudly on the floor.

"They are trying to get me to unlock the door."

"Are you sure they cannot break in and harm you?"

"I don't know. I barricaded it with all the furniture that I had in here." Her voice is trembling; I can sense her terror almost physically.

"Do you want us to stay on the phone? Is this helpful?"

She keeps silent for a second; I can hear her heavy breathing. "Yes, please."

I grab my dressing gown and, headphones in my ears, I go to the kitchen and make some coffee. I have to keep my hands busy to keep the anxiety at bay. The futile routine of making coffee contrasts with the mayhem in a Bangkok hotel room on the other end of the line; it is surreal. But Laila's voice confirms that this is not just a bad dream of mine.

As we sit and talk, her online friends are rushing to attract as much attention as possible to her case. After just a few hours, social media is buzzing with her story, but it is still not enough to reach a high-ranking UN official. She keeps silent for a long moment and I can hear her tapping on her phone, fast and furious. I just stay there, listening to the noises from yet one more room where she has had to lock herself in. I hope this is the last time she has to do that.

Then Laila starts talking. She tells me all about how she has planned for this since the very first day of the lockdown. Her family was scheduled to have a holiday in Turkey and when it was cancelled, she managed to keep the travel authorisation signed by her father. The household was shaken by the lockdown, and the usually steady routine was disrupted as all family members had more time on their hands. With Ramadan starting a few days before, Laila knew that this was the right time for her to attempt the escape. The impending marriage, which now seemed inescapable, had left her with no other option than to act before the end of the quarantine.

"You have helped me to feel stronger, I have had hope again."

***

That night, those who know Laila are not sleeping. After a few hours of social media frenzy, she finally receives a message from a French journalist.

"He wants me to record a video and post it on social media. To attract more attention."

I see his point. The only images of Laila that are circulating online are blurred and vague; her scream for help has no face yet. But I also know what showing her uncovered face to the whole world would mean for her. Her family would never get over the shame; they would be unforgiving.

"Are you prepared to do this?"

She stays silent for a long moment. I listen to her accelerated breathing; she is hyperventilating.

"Laila, let's try to breathe more slowly, breathe with me."

For a few minutes we are inhaling and exhaling together, finding a shared rhythm.

"I am so scared," she whispers.

"I know you are. I am scared for you too."

"They will kill me."

"Let's make sure they cannot. Do you remember the first time you showed me your face?"

"Yes …"

"You did it then, even though it was risky."

"I did."

A few seconds pass and I finally hear her voice, trembling

but clear. Laila tells the world about who she is and why she has barricaded herself in this room. She asks for asylum. As soon as she is done, the video of her talking to the camera appears in my Twitter feed. Then we both observe how her video makes a storm; it is also taken by this storm and propelled further and further around the virtual world. To watch this happening is fascinating. There is no way back for Laila after this, we both know it.

I suddenly feel exhausted; outside the sun is coming out from behind the sleepy buildings. Paris is waking up, oblivious to what has been happening to Laila that night. I make myself another coffee and take it to the balcony. As I watch the sunrise, Laila is crying, at the other end of the world.

I use my phone again, this time to photograph the sky and the rooftops, bathing in the pink light of pale morning sunshine. As she receives my picture, both of us already know that she will make it.

"I have to go and unlock the door … There is somebody from the United Nations here. Thank you for staying with me."

"Yes, the world is waiting for you outside."

We hang up, and back on my computer screen I watch her march out of the room under the glare of the waiting cameras, towards a future in which she will probably still have to hide for a while. As I contemplate my city slowly returning from a deep and troubled sleep, I hope that the days of locked rooms are over for Laila.

II

Jane

London, UK

By the time Jane returns home, we have both grown tired and mildly frustrated with her therapy progress. She keeps connecting for our erratic sessions from different hotel rooms, various Starbucks of the world and even far-away airports. I never know from which place she will call me next, and this inconsistency rattles me a lot. This up-in-the-air, unpredictable lifestyle has been Jane's reality for more than a decade; she is a freelance journalist living out of her suitcase, covering migration flows, populations fleeing wars and refugee camps. Sometimes, I wonder what Jane's deeper reason for being in therapy is. She mutters something about her anxiety and I am left with my questions again, free to guess and no clear answer, at least not yet.

The fast-spreading COVID pandemic finds Jane back in London where she is crashing on her friend's couch, preparing for her next assignment which was meant to take her to South Sudan. With her departure to Africa delayed, Jane makes the hasty decision to go back to Scotland to spend the lockdown at her parents' house in her native village.

After all, she needs rest and sleep, and there she has at least a decent-sized room and has no need to cook or do her own washing.

Jane is resolved to recover from years of not sleeping enough or sleeping in all kinds of uncomfortable or unsafe surroundings. I secretly hope that this forced stop to her peregrinations will help us to catch our breath in therapy too.

When I suggest that we continue our sessions during lockdown, Jane reluctantly agrees, but I already doubt that this will happen.

Several months into her therapy, I still know nearly nothing about Jane's hometown or her childhood. Not only has she been avoiding these topics with determination and skill, but also her crisis-fuelled life has been providing us with plenty of other, more urgent matters to attend to. Jane has been busy surviving dangerous situations, under constant pressure. Fearless and always ready to accept a new assignment, Jane is a good journalist and always seems to be in high demand.

I sit in front of my screen waiting for Jane and I am slightly anxious as I know that she will not be able to hide from her past any more: in her childhood home, it will certainly find a way to catch up with her. I have never been to Scotland and have always dreamed of going, so now I am excited almost as if Jane were taking me there with her.

When she finally logs in, the image on my screen is out of focus – she is using her iPad as usual. "The connection is pretty bad here, not much better than what we are used to," she announces, warning me already about the imperfection of her hometown. Despite her words, her face is now clear on my screen; this is the very first time I can see her so well.

Jane's back-at-home version is wearing an old, oversized white T-shirt, which makes her thin arms look girlish. She looks exhausted; her usual energy, fuelled with anxiety and work pressure, has gone or been left behind in London.

"Since I came back I have not been sleeping well, it is too quiet

… I forgot about how eerie it can get here," she complains. Dark circles under her blue eyes confirm this.

With the lockdown, the coastal village, emptied of the usual flow of tourists, has fallen into despair. The closure of the restaurants has put fishermen out of work for the time being. With the pubs shut, the atmosphere is grim. Jane's own work is frozen, as the western world suddenly became uninterested in dramas happening elsewhere. What is happening here is consuming all our attention, resources and capacity to care. How does Jane feel about this? "Angry, very angry," and as soon as the word 'anger' has been uttered out loud, something shifts; a knot that was growing in my stomach releases ever so slightly. But Jane is not ready to let too much emotion either out or in, and retreats quickly back to her protective anxiety-filled shell. Is there anything else that may explain her sleepless nights at home? Jane is not volunteering much, so I am left guessing again.

"I hate doing this from home," Jane states grimly, her irritation growing. Almost as a reaction to her words, a rumbling noise erupts from the bowels of the house. Jane turns away from the camera and towards the door, off-screen to me. Now I can clearly distinguish the door's trembling and dogs' barking. "Sorry. Wait a sec," Jane jumps up leaving her iPad (with me inside) behind, but has no time to reach the door before two big black dogs burst loudly into the room. For several seconds I am watching Jane scream and push angrily, trying to get rid of the growling intruders. Finally she is able to expel them and locks the door before returning to face me.

"Nasty beasts," she puffs. "There is no way of avoiding them here."

"What are they?"

"Belgian Shepherds … my parents are obsessed with them," she moves her iPad, showing me the rest of the room and I can spot a large, uncannily realistic picture of the same black dogs hanging just above the single bed.

"When I go to sleep, I have to turn it to face the wall … I can't stand it." Jane looks genuinely upset. "They are not completely unfriendly … but there is something creepy about them. My father named them Shock and Shuck, can you believe it?" Jane shrugs in disgust.

"When did it start, your parents' obsession with dogs?"

"I don't remember exactly … a long time ago, I was maybe thirteen or so when they got their first dog."

We sit in silence for a while as Jane seems to be transported back to the time when dogs had not been part of the family. Her gaze is vacant and I wait for her to recollect her memories. Our hour is almost up and I will have to wait to ask my next burning question.

***

When I see Jane again, the neat image of our previous session is gone, and she is back to the blurred, shaky self that I am used to seeing on my screen. She is cramped in the driver's seat of a car, parked outside her parents' house which I spot in the background – a fairy-tale stone cottage tucked up among dozens of blossoming blue hydrangea shrubs.

"I had to get out of there," she explains hastily, fidgeting in the small space of her Mini. She must have been sitting in the car for a while, as the windows are getting steamed up. Outside it is pouring, exactly as pictured in the television crime series set in this part of the British Isles. I can hear the pitter-patter of the rain falling on the car's soft-top. Her hair is wet as if she had to run through the rain to get to her newest therapy room.

"I don't know if I will make it here for much longer," Jane continues, "but I just don't know where else to go." Her nomadic lifestyle has not led to many well-settled friends owning cosy guest rooms. She looks worn down and very young; I have never seen her this low, not even during her toughest assignments, when outside of her tent a reverberation from an explosion would reach us, interrupting the session and forcing Jane to shield in an underground bunker.

"Staying here drives me mad … I feel completely trapped in this house."

"Is that what made you leave years ago?"

Jane left home as soon as she could, eager to extend the limits of her world. Her parents had never travelled and her only childhood experience of tourism was a two-week school trip to Paris, from which she returned with a firm plan to move abroad as soon as high school was over and done with. She still remembers how free and light she felt when, with her best friend, they walked along the large boulevards filled with elegantly dressed people, who sat on the sunbathed terraces and looked oddly happy. During those few days in Paris the girls felt happy too, and free as never before … "And probably never after," Jane adds, as she gets lost in her memories, a nostalgic smile on her pale lips.

My own school trip to Paris fast-forwards in my mind. The same sense of freedom and lightness never experienced in my Soviet childhood tainted by endless dark winters, probably not that dissimilar from Scottish ones, the same decision to move there that I stubbornly turned into reality a few years later.

"Do you think there is any connection between those days in Paris and the fact that years later you ended up with a Parisian therapist?"

Jane smiles: "I haven't thought about that, but yes, probably…"

A loud barking brings us back to the rainy garden and the German Shepherds appear from nowhere and start jumping around the car, growling.

"Oh no, I hoped they would not come back so quickly," Jane, visibly nervous, looks around. "My father must not be far either; he took the dogs on a walk to the cliffs …"

Stressed by the barking that makes it impossible for us to continue, we leave it there. Jane is nervous and eager to retreat to her room. As soon as we disconnect, an energetic knock at the door brings me back to my own lockdown reality. My daughter storms into my office brandishing her phone, eager to resume a never-ending conversation.

"Mum, look at these puppies …" She has been fixated on wanting a dog for a few months now, but with the lockdown, her only-child status, already weighing on her, has become much heavier.

"Why do you really want a dog?" I wonder out loud.

"To have somebody with me when you and Daddy are working … You are both working all the time."

I feel a pang of guilt, but push on with my enquiry as the therapist in me takes over the mother.

"If I had a dog, I could stop thinking about the virus or other scary stuff," she finally delivers. As I hug my daughter, who is mourning this unattainable pet, I'm still thinking about Jane's parents' obsession. "If I had a dog, I could stop thinking about the scary stuff," my daughter's voice resonates in my head.

***

Next time we connect, Jane is in her car again; her phone is placed in a holder and the image is steady. She looks even more exhausted than the previous time.

"I am hungover," Jane announces flatly. Drinking has always been

22

the escape route that Jane takes when things became unmanageable or out of control. There is something rebellious and stubborn in her voice, which reminds me of my teenage daughter again.

"Last time we met, you mentioned that you were thirteen when your parents' obsession with dogs started…" Jane nods, slightly surprised by my question. "Do you remember what was going on in your family at that time?" I see Jane's face freezing, which confirms that we are on to something. She stays silent for several long seconds, then turns away from the camera, looks outside in the direction of the cottage.

"Let's get out of here." She turns the key, which was already in the ignition and, before I can protest, the Mini takes off. This is the first time a patient takes me for a drive!

"I will show you around."

As Jane accelerates down the village road, I observe her face, unable to read her expression. Determination? Anger? Fear? Anxiety? I am not sure. The noise of the engine and the speed with which we are leaving behind the small houses, the trees, make me realise that we are going fast. In a few minutes the sudden change of light confirms that we are now on the coastal road. I can spot the silvery sea shimmering on Jane's right, when the car makes a particularly sharp turn.

A road trip session is certainly not a mainstream modality, and I am losing all control over what is going on. Any semblance of therapeutic boundaries or the sanctity of the therapy room has been stretched to vanishing point. Jane is the one in the driving seat, and I suddenly realise that she can launch her car off the cliff, taking me with her, and I will be unable to do anything to prevent this from happening. I have no option but to wait, hoping that she has an agenda, and it is not a suicide in the company of her online therapist.

"Jane, how far are we going?"

"To the cliffs. You will see; it's beautiful there."

Soon enough Jane stops the car and switches off the engine. As she opens the top of her Mini, the sound of the waves fills my small office. She stays in her seat, looking in front of her, mesmerised, and I hold my breath.

"I have not been back here in twenty years ... It has not changed."

She unfastens her seatbelt, takes the phone out of the holder, opens the door, and gets us out of the car. The wind makes her blonde hair fly, and now I can barely hear her speaking: "Let's go for a walk."

Jane is on a mission now and I am suddenly terrified for her. From what I can see, the landscape looks wild and completely deserted. The reddish cliffs covered by wild flowers are high. Jane takes a few steps and finally stops at the edge. She seems to have forgotten all about me and the phone is unsteady in her hand. The sound of the waves gets louder. I am relieved that her earphones have not been blown away by the wind.

"Jane, what happened here when you were thirteen?" My voice brings her back and she looks into the camera, her eyes wide. "Maybe we should return to the car, it is getting too windy here," I say, my fear growing as she takes another step towards the edge. She stays silent, ignoring my suggestion, then utters almost inaudibly: "Mary ..."

"Jane, I am here. Let's go back to the car and sit."

Finally, to my relief, she obeys and turns around. Once back to the safety of the Mini, she puts the phone down on the passenger seat, and the only thing I can now see is the blue Scottish sky with a few idyllic fluffy clouds chased by the wind. I cannot see Jane any more, but her breathing and sobbing are clearly audible in my earphones.

"Jane, who is Mary?"

"My sister … My twin sister."

"What happened to her here?"

"She fell off the cliff."

Jane's sobbing is getting more desperate, as I have to stay with the view of the sky and the blowing of the wind. For a second I miss the old-style therapy room, in which she would sit in front of me in a comfortable armchair, just a few feet away (not a safe distance by current standards), and I would be able to offer her a tissue, a glass of water or even a hug.

When she is finally able to speak again, she picks up the phone and puts it back into the holder. Her face, red and wet with tears, reappears on my screen.

"Sorry," she says in her unmistakably Scottish accent. She is now ready to tell me her story.

Jane and Mary fought like cats and dogs all through their childhood. They were identical to the point that even their parents were unable to distinguish between them; the only times they would get along was when they were resolved to play a 'twin prank' on their family or friends. "I always felt that when she was around, I had no space, no right to exist."

The day of their thirteenth birthday the sisters received the gift they had been demanding for years – two puppies from the same litter. Jane loved her puppy at first sight. The puppies were certainly another desperate attempt by their parents to appease the twins' tumultuous relationship.

Several weeks later, in the early morning, Jane found her puppy dead in her bed.

"Maybe you squashed it to death in your sleep?" suggested her sister. Their parents' choice of dogs with two very different coats did not leave room for any doubt about whose dog had died. That day Jane cried her eyes out. Mary was pretending to be sad, but Jane knew too well that her twin could not bear seeing her happy. Did Mary kill her puppy and put it in her bed? She could not be sure and was trying hard to convince herself that her sister was not *that* evil. Their parents did their best to console her, but when they promptly offered to get another puppy, Jane declined; she did not want a new dog, she was already attached to this one and mourning her premature loss.

A week after the incident, their mother insisted on a family outing; they all needed a distraction. It was a cloudless, sunny day, and while their parents were preparing the picnic, the girls ran around playing with the puppy that they were now instructed to share.

As they were far enough from their parents, Mary did everything to make sure that her sister understood that the surviving dog was hers and hers alone.

"Then she looked me in the eyes and announced bluntly that she was the one who killed my puppy." Jane's voice was trembling with hatred. "I could not stand it any longer and I pushed her hard … We fell onto the grass and fought, as we never had before …" Mary had always been the stronger of them; she was the first-born, and Jane knew that she stood no chance against her sister when it came to a physical fight. At some point, when she managed to escape her sister's strong arms, Jane ran away and started to climb the cliffs. Mary chased her, but Jane was faster and more agile, and all she wanted was to find a safe place to hide … The next thing she remembered was the terrible scream as her sister fell.

When she looked back, Mary was not there anymore. She approached the edge and looking down, saw her twin's body being thrown against the rocks by the waves. From afar it looked as if the sea was playing with a human-size doll.

The rest of the day was all a blur. Her parents screamed and cried, and the fire fighters and the police arrived at some point. Jane was brought back home, and questioned several times by a female police officer. The conclusion was that Mary had had a terrible accident. Jane inherited the puppy, which quickly grew into a dog, but she could not love him as he reminded her of her double loss.

Jane tells me her whole story in one long monologue, as if she was scared that I would not let her finish. When she finally stops, our fifty minutes have turned into an hour and a half, and we both feel hollowed out by her revelation. Again, the traditional 'boundaries' have fallen by the wayside.

"Jane, what happened to you and your sister is terrible." I can hardly find the words that would be enough. "But none of this was your fault." I guess that nobody had ever told her these simple words that she so desperately needed.

"The worst part is that I did not feel any regret. I was not even sad. It was just an enormous relief not to have her around anymore. And my parents always knew it; I am sure they still wonder whether I pushed her off that cliff …"

We sit together for some time in silence, considering Jane's last statement, and I believe that she is probably right, and her parents have been living with the suspicion that their only remaining daughter is a murderer.

"Did you discuss it with them?"

"No, never," Jane sighs. "Nobody talks about it; they simply pretend that they never had another daughter."

Jane reassures me that she will return home and rest. We agree to resume our conversation the next day. I am left in front of my empty screen trying to process what has just happened.

***

After she died, Mary was never spoken about, her name never mentioned. As they were indistinguishable from each other, their parents only had pictures in which only one of the twins was present, pretending that it was Jane. The people in the village seemed to just go along with their denial, as it was easier than finding the words to speak about their loss. Mary-fallen-from-the-cliff was an uncomfortable member of the family to live with.

Sometimes Jane would catch her mother watching her with a terrified look, struggling for an answer to her unspeakable question. After a while she started wondering herself what had really happened on that cliff. She remembered so well the hatred she felt, when Mary told her about killing the puppy. The nightmares of her twin strangling the puppy had haunted her for years, until she was finally able to replace them with other images of killings and dead bodies that she was reporting on.

For Jane, bringing me to the place of her family drama was probably the only way to tell her deeply buried story. She took me to that cliff to make me an eyewitness to her sister's death. I had to look where her parents had averted their gaze. Jane's earlier choice of an online therapist had an obvious reason – her mobile and stressful lifestyle – but at a deeper level, it was this opportunity to take me back home that perhaps played a bigger role.

***

The next day we resume and Jane surprises me with new scenery again: I see her sitting on a bench surrounded by the rocks. I can hear the sound of waves crashing against the rocks, and almost smell the salty wind still blowing in her hair from the sea.

"I found this." She presents a thick blue notebook to the camera. Following our previous session she asked her mother whether they had kept any of her sister's belongings. Her mother avoided looking her in the eye, did not utter a word, but went straight to her bedroom and returned with the notebook, pleading: "But, please, do not tell your father. He does not know I kept it."

Jane had no idea that her sister kept a diary. She spent another sleepless night reading through its pages. Mary had written in her diary every single day for the whole year leading to her death.

"Can I read you some passages?" she asks and I nod in approval. Jane starts to read: "When I look at HER, I have the impression that I cannot exist. Having her around kills me. She takes all the space. I want HER to disappear from this house, from my life."

In the distorted mirror of her twin's words, Jane recognised her own thoughts, amplified by Mary's troubled mind. Jane always felt ashamed that such thoughts even crossed her mind; she remembers praying in bed for hours, trying to chase them out of her head. Did the hatred that she felt at times towards her sister belong to her, or was it just a pale reflection of what was going on inside her twin's head?

When Jane resumes her reading, her voice is almost inaudible, she sounds like a little girl: "Yesterday I found HER puppy dead on the kitchen floor. It was still warm. I had the idea of putting it in her bed, under the covers. I watched HER sleeping, because I wanted to be there and see her face when she discovered it. I even made HER believe she did it!" Jane stops reading, tears in her eyes.

"She was not evil but she was so unwell …" Then she looks straight into the camera seeking my confirmation of her sister's mental struggle. "How come no one noticed?" she wonders. Her parents had to know. They had read the diary after all. Living with a child fallen from a cliff, probably pushed by her sibling was uncomfortable enough, but living with a child who was 'crazy' was probably not much better.

"They are so ashamed." Jane finally names the feeling that had infiltrated their family long ago. Shame had muted them all, breaking links, killing any hope for healing.

The year following her sister's death, Jane was sent to boarding school. Her parents could not bear looking at her any more, as she was a constant reminder of their loss. Her presence triggered their shame about the conflict between their twins that they were not able to resolve and had resulted in Mary's death. At boarding school, Jane almost forgot about Mary, pushing her to the very back of her mind. There, nobody knew that she ever had a twin sister. Sometimes, Mary would take her revenge by appearing in Jane's dreams, turning them into dreadful nightmares, which would leave her petrified for days.

As we progress, her parents' obsession with dogs becomes less of a mystery too. Dogs offered them an easy topic to turn their attention to, and a safe thing to talk about. Jane often saw them sunk into the deep armchairs of their dark sitting room, each of them stroking a dog's massive head and discussing endlessly dog-related topics – pet food, walks, veterinary appointments. They were rehearsing their dog-related talk for the next time they bumped into a neighbour; these conversations would always follow a well-established order: weather first, dogs second.

As long as her parents have their pets, they can avoid their unbearable shame. By returning home for the lockdown, Jane has been threatening the defence system elaborated by her parents and guarded by their dogs.

"Maybe I should talk to them?" she asks, and we both know that she does not need my answer.

***

When we meet again a week later, Jane is back to the relative safety of her car. The convertible's top is closed, despite the sun shining; her packed suitcase is visible on the back seat.

"I am heading back to London after the session," she announces. "There is nothing to be done." I can sense her disappointment, echoed by my own. "When I brought up Mary, my father got angry and stormed out of the house," she continues, as I make a mental note that at least she managed to speak up. "My mother kept her mouth shut, as usual."

Her parents' shame about the past overrides their love for their only remaining daughter. Do they realise that they are probably losing her forever?

"They have their dogs and seem pretty content."

"And what about you?"

"I have my work … and now also this," she brandishes her sister's diary in front of the camera, then returns it to the passenger's seat. "You know … this is the first time that I have felt sad about Mary's death."

"Have you done everything you needed to do here?" Jane considers my question for a long minute, and then she turns away from the camera and looks at her childhood home with its idyllic façade serving to keep their family drama away from sight.

"When I brought up my sister's name, I was looking at my father …" Jane was blown away by the intensity of the old man's emotions: his face went red, then dropped as he was overtaken by rage. He screamed at his daughter: "Do not talk about HER!" before storming out, followed by the dogs' barking.

"If only they could talk about Mary …" Since her twin's remains had been recovered from the sea and buried in a closed casket, nobody had ever spoken her name.

"I am not sure I would even be able to find her grave in the cemetery."

The day of the burial, as the young Jane stood frozen, looking at the dark hole in the ground swallowing her sister's body, she felt a sudden feeling of emptiness descending on her, as if half of her was gone forever. This emptiness stayed with her, and nothing could change that – not friendship, not sex and not adventure. With her twin gone, Jane lost her tormenter but also any hope of resolving their conflict, or of learning how to be in a relationship without being hurt and betrayed. She remained trapped in that last fight that the two of them had just a few seconds before Mary's tragic fall. As a result, Jane stayed away from anybody who could offer her any kind of closeness. How could she believe in a relationship as a peaceful place, free of persecution and threat?

"The other day I dreamt of Mary again … for the first time in years … She was trying to catch me, exactly like that last time. But when I looked back, I suddenly realised that what she really wanted from me was a hug. And that's when I woke up." Her eyes wide open, Jane stares in front of her, seemingly into the car's rear view mirror. Is she looking for Mary in her own reflection?

"How did you feel when you woke up?"

"My heart was racing and I felt terribly sad … because that hug never happened." Jane looks away from the mirror and starts crying silently.

"If you could say something to your sister now, what would it be?" Jane shrugs, her tears falling freely now. Then she returns to the mirror and utters, "I did not know that you were suffering so much … I am so sorry." Jane's tears become full-blown sobbing.

We are interrupted by a knock on the window; I can spot somebody standing outside the car. Jane, surprised by this intrusion, turns white: "Mum?"

"Sorry, just a second," she mumbles, then leaves her earphones on the seat and gets out of the car. The door slams and I can only wait

32

for Jane to return. What are they saying to each other? I am deprived of any control again, unable to see what is going on outside the car, where I am stuck alone. Their conversation takes only a few minutes, which seems very long from my side of the screen.

As soon as Jane returns, she turns the key and the car starts moving slowly. As she is manoeuvring out of the driveway, for a second I can spot her mother's silhouette waving to us. "It will be quick, promise," Jane volunteers.

"What about your mother?"

"She told me that she always knew that Mary was very ill, but my father did not want to hear anything about a psychiatrist ..." Her mother knew that it was hell for Jane to be around her sister, so when Mary fell from the cliff, her first thought was that Jane could not take it any longer and had pushed her sister off the cliff. "When I told her that it was an accident, she was so relieved ... We ended up hugging, the first time in years."

Jane stops the car. When she gets out, she takes her phone with her. "Please, come with me," she asked as if I had much of a choice. I can hear Jane walking on gravel as we pass trees and a few stone crosses. After a few steps she stops: "This is where Mary is buried."

We say our goodbyes and I leave her alone at her sister's grave.

"Thank you for coming home with me" are her last words.

"I am glad I did." And I mean it.

III

Alan

Manhattan, New York

"I am in a terrible dilemma ..."

With his striped Italian shirt, Alan, neatly shaven and perfectly groomed, sounds like a soap opera character. His eyes, as blue as his shirt, look tired.

Alan is a high-ranking officer in the New York Police Department. During his lunch break, he has locked himself into his top-floor office in Manhattan to connect with me for our very first session. In Paris, it is already dusk and he is my last client of the day.

"At least I will not bump into a colleague from the bureau at your front door," he explains with a charming smile. Indeed he will not; our offices are thousands of miles apart. I realise that Alan has considered all his options before going for an online therapist from far away. With my European accent, I probably sound exotic to him. When I ask, he shrugs, eager to move on to business.

Alan's troubles started a year ago, when Chloe burst into his then well-organised and contented married life. They met at Alan's yacht club, where she was working as a bartender. Since then, his existence has been divided into two parts neatly separated by the East River, and this situation has grown increasingly intolerable.

Alan must find a solution to his dilemma, and my clearly stated task is to help him take the right decision, choosing between his wife and his lover. It sounds like a clearly defined job, but something rattles me from inside; I do not believe that this is all there is to it.

As I listen to Alan describing his situation in a measured way, I can spot behind him a striped white and green flag alongside his department's motto – *Fidelis ad Mortem* (Faithful till Death) – an ironic reminder of his current conflict.

Our first hour is entirely dedicated to his praising both women's unquestionable virtues. Alan keeps talking and I imagine an Alan-child in a sweet shop presented with too many choices.

Alan's wife is a medical doctor. They have a nice penthouse in East Village and two French bulldogs. "I know I should be a happy man." Alan's attempt to persuade me does not work. He does not look convinced either.

"Tell me more about your marriage." I try to refocus on the relationship rather than the characters of Alan's drama.

"My wife is a strong woman. I admire her, respect her, but …" Alan is not fooled easily; he keeps on his tracks, well polished by a year of ruminating.

"What kind of relationship do you have?"

My question takes Alan by surprise. Is there such thing as a relationship with sweets? "We are good. We make a perfect crew, I guess." Alan is into sailing, and here we are talking about the boat he has been actively rocking for the last year. Something in Alan invites sarcasm. I struggle to join him in his place of emotional torture. And yet tortured he feels.

"What about your relationship with Chloe then?"

As soon as I pronounce the magic spell of his lover's name, Alan's face lights up: "She is such a breath of fresh air."

But I am not sure he can live with so much fresh air without catching a chill; Alan seems used to the cosiness of his relationship with his reliable wife.

"Alan, but what did you mean when you referred to 'a perfect crew'?" I acknowledge my lack of sailing references.

"Trusting each other to do the right thing, I guess …"

"Do you trust yourself to do the right thing?"

"I used to, at least at work. But now … no, not any more …"

I wait for a few long seconds, watching the gloomy waves of doubt transpiring through Alan's skin. "I actually doubt it strongly," he admits, and a few drops of sweat appear on his suntanned forehead.

"What makes you doubt?"

"Chloe …"

I will not hear more about Chloe today, as our time is up.

As Alan's face leaves my screen, my own past takes over, and a familiar face fades in – the same inescapable charm, the same restless blue eyes … Andrey was my teenage crush. Ten years my senior, he chose to become a policeman, a career that I dreamed about while at high school. For several years our relationship dithered on the thin edge between romance and friendship. The latter eventually won, and the complicity we then shared still makes me smile today. Andrey died two decades ago, caught up in a complex, thriller-like enquiry into drug trafficking. He was shot in an ambush set up by his corrupt colleagues. His idealism and righteousness were incompatible with their practices and the blurred boundaries between police and crime during the immediate post-Soviet anarchy.

Andrey's ghost has been sleeping in some dark corner of my mind but is now awakened by Alan, and I watch him making himself comfortable in one of the armchairs reserved for the clients who come to my office in Paris. He winks at me in that unique manner that made my teenage heart go faster, and lights up a cigarette, but I can hardly protest.

I make sure the door of my office is firmly shut before I join my family in the living room next door. Working from an office in the family apartment is obviously practical, but it also comes with thinner boundaries between the two areas of my life.

***

I do not hear from Alan for another few weeks; his dilemma is already fading from my memory when he suddenly makes another appointment to see me.

This time, his whole body looks a mess (or at least the upper part that I can see on my screen). In striking contrast to the first time we met, he does not jump straight in but stays silent for a few seconds, an uneasy smile on his weary face. "I really need you to help me figure this out ..." He has not been sleeping well for a few months now, but over these recent weeks his insomnia has worsened. Usually a fast decision-maker, he is stuck this time.

"Why can I not just make a decision? What is wrong with me?", he keeps repeating his mantra, bewildered by his own inability to come up with the right answer.

When a client is stuck, ironically the best way forward is often backwards. So we start exploring Alan's past; trying to find something that would explain his current drama. At first he resists my attempts: "What does it have to do with my parents?" Introspection does not come easily or naturally to him. His parents, two emigrant kids who became a policeman and a nurse, did not indulge much in self-reflection.

Alan does give in after a while and starts collaborating; he tries hard to remember, share and think. He talks about his father, who spent his working life in the police department, patrolling his neighbourhood. He was 'a straight shooter', Alan smiles, and I feel touched by the pride he shows in his father. His mother, now retired, dedicated her time to caring for her elderly patients at the local nursing home. Both worked night shifts, which often left their son alone, responsible for his younger sister. His parents always praised Alan for being a good boy, a big boy, even when he was only seven. At that age he was able to feed his toddler sister, put her to bed, as well as himself, and read her a story. They did very well together, a well-organised little team. With his family values of hard work, Alan turned into a perfect little soldier, at work and at home.

For years, his sister was his closest friend; he helped her throughout the agony of her teenage years, her first love disappointments and her high school exams. Alan took his older brother role seriously, so when she grew up and moved abroad to teach English, he felt abandoned. Every time he mentions his sister, his face lightens up and looks younger, unguarded.

**

With every session Alan grows more fidgety, his usual self-containment slowly crumbling into pieces. I soon start doubting as well. Am I able to offer him what he really needs?

"How are you feeling today?"

"Same as usual …" We have been there together exactly twelve times – the number of hours that I have spent so far with Alan and his two women. I am getting familiar with both of them: the strong-willed, hard-working wife, 'a monument to pride', and the 'breath of fresh air', bubbly Chloe.

"Torn, lost, confused." Alan's capacity for introspection is developing, but we do not seem to get any closer to the decision that he desperately wants. An overwhelming sense of futility swamps us both, and I want to give up and have to resist a powerful temptation to just switch off and claim a loss of connection.

"What would happen if you gave up, if you just stopped trying so hard to figure this out?" I ask out of desperation.

"I don't know ..." Alan looks panicked; he has been struggling with this dilemma for too long. "I just want to do the right thing."

Doing the right thing has always been imperative for Alan, but this time, maybe the very first time in his life, he realises that there is no 'right decision' to solve his problem. Whichever way he chooses, he hurts a woman he loves.

"Have you ever felt in the past a similar pressure to take the right decision?"

Alan stays silent for a while, his eyes wandering to the New York skyline in the window. "Yes, actually, I have."

We are onto something ...

"My father ... a few years before his passing, we had a conversation ..." Alan starts recollecting his memories; I can barely breathe. "I had just finished at the police academy and was back home after graduation. He took me to Ciro, his old friend's trattoria, to celebrate. As we ate his favourite spaghetti alle vongole, he told me that he had cancer. But this was not why he wanted to talk ... He wanted to tell me that he had another woman in his life, Maria ... They had been seeing each other for years. 'I am very attached to your mother but I love Maria. I am worried about your mother, she may take it badly' ... He wanted me to make the right decision for him."

As Alan speaks, the whole scene plays out in front of me: the young Alan in his brand new uniform; his retired father, exhausted by a life torn between work and two women; the warm atmosphere of an old trattoria; its large white tablecloths; rich garlicky smells from the kitchen, and a bottle of red Sicilian wine on the table. The celebratory lunch where a father tries to pass his terrible dilemma onto his son.

The scene has a fascinating, almost cinematic quality.

Now Alan is seeking from me the very thing that his father wanted from him– somebody to share the burden of his responsibility.

"And what was your response?"

"I was shocked … then furious. I stormed out and did not see him for a few weeks."

"And did he tell your mother in the end?"

"I don't know … I don't think so. His cancer was worse than he thought, he declined quickly after this … My mother cared for him until the very end."

It is only in therapy that Alan had ever spoken about his father's affair. In sharing this burden with me, he feels relieved, but putting Maria's existence into words also makes her more real.

"Have you asked your mother about Maria?"

"No, I could not …" Alan reveals he was too scared of hearing that his mother had known about it.

"And what about Maria?"

"I never met her. My father did not talk about her again … Sometimes I wonder whether that conversation ever happened."

"And your father's dilemma was never properly resolved …"

We sit in silence, listening to the echoes of his father's story. The old man is with us, and I can almost sense the smell of his tobacco penetrating my office (he was a regular smoker), unless it is just my neighbour enjoying a cigarette on the balcony beneath my open window. Or, is it Andrey's invisible ghost, lighting up again?

"I didn't think about my father that much until now … and here I am, in a similar situation."

"Why do you think your father decided to tell you about his cancer and his affair at the same time?"

"I have no idea … Maybe he wanted to soften the pain of one with the shock of the other … And it actually worked. I was troubled. Realising that my father, with all his family values, attending church every Sunday, could have an affair, I completely overlooked the fact that he was actually dying."

At his father's funeral, where hundreds of colleagues and friends from the police department gathered, Alan was torn between the pride he felt for his father's reputation and the shame about his secret affair. He could not help closely watching his mother receiving condolences in a solemn and dignified manner, trying to catch any hint on whether she knew too.

He was also looking suspiciously at any woman on her own, trying to guess whether Maria was there. He was so absorbed in his surveillance that, at the end of that day, he could hardy remember the many words that his father's friends had said to him.

"Alan, it was very unfortunate for your father to die without sorting out his personal life. But it is even more unfortunate for you to have inherited his dilemma. It is not your job to solve this for him."

Alan leaves the session visibly shaken but uplifted. In front of my screen, I am left with my own questions about this. Did his mother know about her husband's affair all along? Was Maria for real, or was she just the old man's way of avoiding a lengthy conversation with his son about death approaching?

Before leaving my office, I notice that the armchair in which Andrey's ghost sat the other day is empty, but a very faint smell of cigarettes is floating in the air despite the closed window.

***

Alan

The next time we reconnect, Alan is in control again, with his back straight, as if during this past week somebody has reorganised his whole body. I am taken aback, disoriented for a split second, and already missing the more imperfect and relatable version of Alan.

"I have now made my decision, but prefer to run it by you first, and this session should be our last."

I suddenly feel like one of his operatives, preparing for a critical intelligence meeting. I am straightening my back too.

"You were right. I kept thinking about what you said about my wife being like my mother … and me trying to protect her from my father's affair, by sticking with her …" [Did I ever say this?] "Now is the time for me to mind my own business."

It looks like, in his self-reorganisation process, Alan overlooked some pieces of his personality, or did he leave them aside on purpose? This new absence of doubt turns Alan into a flattened character, some cartoonish version of a handsome cop from a TV series from the 1980s.

"I am leaving my wife. With Chloe I feel that I am doing the right thing again."

"OK, and what is it about her that makes you feel this way?"

"She is so driven … I used to be like that when I joined the NYPD. Now I feel deflated. Things are not what they seemed." Saying this, Alan gives a theatrical glimpse at his watch to let me know that he is done with the session that has just started, and actually with his therapy.

I feel irritated with him for dumping his disappointment with his work onto me at the last minute and leaving it there, unaddressed.

The resolution of Alan's dilemma falls flat; the tension dissipates, taking the magic away from the space between us.

We both feel ready to part. Alan thanks me warmly, praising my professionalism, and switches off.

I stare at my empty screen; unsure whether I should celebrate the satisfaction of my client or bemoan a failure. Alan came to me hoping to resolve his dilemma, and so he did, according to him. This ending sounds good enough, but inside of me the stubborn little voice of my intuition is whispering that it has been a far too easy denouement. I know the sound of this voice too well to pretend that it may be wrong.

I turn off my computer and, stretching my back, sore from all the sitting in front of the screen, I turn around to face my personal ghost – Andrey is back in his armchair, looking at me ironically and smoking again. Does he want to tell me something?

"Things are not what they seemed." It is actually Alan's voice that resonates in my head. What if the romantic dilemma was only a red herring and I completely overlooked what was really troubling Alan? Now it is too late to ask, Alan has stopped his therapy, I have to grapple with this question alone. For the first time I feel the pain of Andrey's absence.

***

After a couple of weeks, my fleeting thoughts about Alan and his now happily resolved dilemma have been overtaken by other clients' problems. Paris and most of the world have suddenly been locked down to contain the spread of a seemingly unbeatable virus. This new uncanny world becomes the perfect backdrop for countless human dramas, as in a masterfully staged play. My practice is quickly engulfed by these concurrent dramas and I struggle to stay afloat.

***

44

Alan

A few days into the lockdown, reading the news, I am scrolling through the troubling images of an emptied New York, and Alan comes to mind, just as my inbox buzzes with a new email: Alan wants to talk again and it is urgent.

Here I am again, waiting in front of my screen for Alan to connect, as planned. He is running late for the first time. Outside, the initially timid spring has suddenly turned warm; my office is getting hot; birds are loud. I feel an instant urge to switch off the computer and flee to the open air – not an unusual feeling for an online therapist stuck in front of a screen, now amplified by the imposed need to stay indoors.

Alan's call drags me back to the room.

His face is distorted by agony again. These transformations have marked his therapy progress so far.

"I cannot leave Cathy … not now, not in the middle of this." This is the first time Alan calls his wife by her first name. Cathy's hospital is becoming overloaded with patients affected by the virus. Ambulances are queuing outside to bring in more and more of them. The situation is deteriorating quickly; there is not enough protective gear, not enough ventilators … Alan tells me about all these things that I have read about in the news. His wife's everyday drama, so vivid and real, has overtaken his own struggle, making it smaller, changing its scale in just a few days.

"She is risking her life to do the right thing, and I …"

Life has thrown him back into the dark abyss of uncertainty.

What about Chloe? She remains on her own in her small apartment. They had just celebrated Alan's decision. He had brought champagne and a symbolic toothbrush, now left unused on her sink, alongside her own. The lockdown has put their project on hold.

On the other side of the East river, and on my Paris screen, Alan is frightened for his wife.

The juxtaposition of love and death is a familiar theme from his childhood. His mother used to talk about her declining patients as she came back home after her shift. She was very fond of some of them; and Alan is still able to recite their names – Mrs Donaldson, Ms Torelli, the dear Mr Granata … They were an invisible but constant presence in the household; their frail figures turning up as benevolent ghosts at any moment of a family gathering. Sometimes his father would get mad at his wife: 'Smettila con i tuoi vecchi!' (Enough with your old people!), but she would ignore him, and continue to bring home souvenirs from the dead – an old flowery shawl, a Murano vase, a silver teapot, objects that their own grown-up children did not want, and had left to her, a memory of a passed life, a tangible proof of their existence. During the thirty years of her employment at the nursing home, Alan's mother was constantly going to funerals, saying countless goodbyes, but he never saw her cry; her grief was light, as if death was nothing for her but a natural part of life and, as such, had to be celebrated equally.

At the very end of the session, as we are about to say goodbye, a clamour of clapping hands resonates into my office through the open window. On the other side of the screen, Alan looks bewildered.

"Parisians are clapping for our health workers every evening at 8," I explain.

"I told Cathy about you the other day … She was surprised that I was seeing a therapist."

"Did she ask you why?"

"No, she did not … but maybe she guessed …"

We leave things again on this uncertain note, and I recall that, as I was already living in Paris, I had not been able to attend Andrey's funeral.

Alan

***

A few long weeks into lockdown, New York is burying its unclaimed Covid dead in common graves on Hart Island. Alan logs into our session from a bench on the street. The city around him remains silent, weighed down by grief and fear. This is the first time I have seen him outside, and as he uses his phone, the image is unstable in his shaky hands. Tucked in a thick leather jacket, Alan's compact figure looks surprisingly small in this surreal landscape.

"Yesterday I walked my dogs along the river bank, I was looking towards Brooklyn, where Chloe was surely waiting for my call, but I just could not call her ... I cannot bear her unhappiness ... She sounds just like my little sister ..."

Transported back to those long nights, when he was on duty, taking care of his sleepless baby sister, Alan feels the heavy weight of his responsibility. She was a frail child, not coping alone, a complicated teenager putting herself in tricky situations. "Go and take care of your sister. She needs protection," his father would instruct. Alan-good-brother had always been there for his sister until she left to work abroad. When Chloe entered Alan's life, he jumped back easily into his familiar big brother role. When I point this substitution to Alan, he frowns.

I watch him sliding back into his old dilemma-ridden place; the speed of this backward movement is astonishing. How can I keep him from slipping down into the familiar trap?

Every time I observe Alan's metamorphosis closely, the two contradicting versions of him keep taking turns on my screen: one is the self-contained, competent man, in charge, and another – a young boy – overwhelmed by too great a responsibility to do the right thing. The first probably knows what the right thing is, but he cannot communicate it to the boy; these two parts of Alan exist in two separate realities.

"How old do you feel right now?"

Surprised, Alan looks at his screen "I have no idea ... young," he admits with an ironic smile. We both know that he is approaching his mid-forties.

I watch the little boy wrestling with the impossible decision and realise that we have focused a lot on the demanding child but not paid much attention to the adult part of Alan.

"Could we imagine for a second that the whole two-women dilemma did not exist?" He nods, unconvinced. "What would be keeping you awake at night then?" We both sit in silence trying to imagine Alan in his bed, unable to find sleep, but not because of Chloe ...

"What might you be thinking about?"

"My job ..."

"And what exactly about your job?" Alan blinks uneasily, uncomfortable with his own thoughts.

"I used to be proud of being a cop. My father taught me how to be one ... It was all about doing the right thing. But now ... sometimes I am not sure I am on the right side of the barricade."

"What do you mean exactly?" At this question something breaks free in him, the flow of his angry and bitter words pours freely, unlocked. He has lost trust in the system. Chloe, a confirmed feminist and activist with the Black Lives Matter movement, brought into his life her young idealistic rebellion against the flaws of society. Being around her makes it impossible to ignore the violence used by his institution against the more vulnerable, as if wearing a uniform was a privilege rather than a duty. The other day Chloe was making a banner with the words: 'Your oath was to protect us, not kill us, and he took it as aimed at him.

"I'm ashamed of being a cop ..."

As Parisians start applauding our health workers again,

marking the end of our session, Alan's face slides off the screen as he bends to stroke his dogs lying at his feet. We are both reminded about his wife, and Alan's shame is palpable, no distance or unstable connection can help him to conceal it.

"I have to go and make something for dinner."

Alan briefly reappears in the video-call frame, a faint smile on his lips. The dogs agitate around him and jump up, trying to lick his face.

After the session, I read the newspaper headlines about the anti-police violence protests that are shaking New York. I scrutinise the images and the sound of many outraged voices fills my room. I see unmasked rioters facing masked policemen, various hand-written signs, I can feel a fierce energy emanating from a colourful crowd, and I catch myself trying to find Chloe among the protestors. I have never seen her, but a young African–American woman is photographed shouting defiantly on the front line – it could be her. I suddenly understand Alan's fascination with Chloe.

Now I am starting to guess what has brought Andrey's ghost back. His personal crisis must have been similar to Alan's, questioning the very profession that used to be a source of meaning and pride in his life. The reality in which Andrey was living was different of course, but his loss of faith in the law enforcement system was similarly troubling and caused his dramatic end.

One dilemma was actually hiding another one. Alan-child has been feeling overwhelmed by his adult responsibilities towards his two women, while Alan-adult has been struggling with a crisis triggered by doubts about his work.

***

Alan connects for our following session from his bedroom and his face tells me right away that something is very wrong. I feel for him instantly – a clear sharp pain in my stomach.

"Cathy got it, she caught the virus."

She was sent home from the hospital with a temperature and is now isolating in their guest room. She has started to cough.

"I called my mother to tell her about Cathy …"

Their conversation did not go the way Alan expected. He startled himself by telling his mother everything about Chloe: their year-old affair, his recent pre-lockdown decision to leave his wife, and his renewed dilemma, amplified by Cathy's illness. The explanation that he had rehearsed for Cathy was delivered to his mother, and the mild catharsis that Alan felt during his monologue caused him embarrassment, as he also knew that he was talking to the wrong woman.

Telling the truth was a liberating experience, but his mother's reaction was even more so. "She insisted that I tell the truth to Cathy. To convince me, she used the example of my father."

So, his father had finally found the strength to come clean with his wife soon after their conversation at the trattoria. Maria was not there at the funeral; she had come to say her goodbyes a few days before his death. Alan's mother had gone to her house and brought her home with her. She recalled: "After Maria and your father spoke, we cried together in the kitchen. She was a good person …"

For all these years, Alan's protection had actually been unnecessary.

"My sister knew about Maria all along." The little sister was coping well with the flawed image of their father, probably more so than Alan himself.

I notice Alan's eyes slipping away from the screen again and again; I guess that he is checking his phone.

Alan

"Alan, what is going on?"

"It's Chloe … She's been arrested at the protests." He is suddenly alert, ready to run and save her. "Sorry, let me reply … I should try and get her out." I watch him typing frantically on his phone. I wait. "She does not want me to help her." He puts his phone down and looks confused.

"Probably she can deal with it herself?"

"That's exactly what she's saying."

"Chloe seems to know what she is doing. What about you?"

"Maybe I should leave my job." When Alan spills out these words, an invisible balloon of tension bursts – I can almost hear a pop. This has clearly been on his mind for a while. Now that Alan verbalises his doubts, everything comes out in one long spiel – his uneasiness with some colleagues' behaviour, certain jokes by the coffee machine and the tacit normalisation of violence in dealing with protesters. Alan's loyalty towards his uniform was such that he avoided the subject altogether, but with Chloe in his life he just couldn't do it any longer.

This is where I have to leave him this time – alone, with his wife suffering in the next room, Chloe detained somewhere in town and a new dilemma expressed about the institution he has embraced for his whole life.

***

Connecting from his bedroom again for our next session, Alan looks feverish, red-eyed.

"It is really bad … Cathy's condition has got worse."

A blue mask hanging round his neck, Alan is sitting on a wooden floor, his back against the unmade bed in which he has been sleeping alone for the past few nights. I can hear Cathy coughing in the other room. The room looks gloomy. I can almost smell the unwashed sheets, the cold coffee, the fear of death. Alan's despair is tangible.

"I still haven't told her about Chloe or about wanting to resign."

"Do you want to?"

"I must. I don't want to lie to her any more … not now."

"What will you say?"

"That I am in love with another woman and was about to leave her … and that I am thinking about leaving my job."

Alan's dilemma is gone. Telling the truth to Cathy is now the right thing to do, although the past tense used by Alan is interesting.

Just before the end of the session, Alan stands up, leaving his phone on the floor, without disconnecting. I can hear his steps down the corridor, a door opening slowly, and Alan's faint voice. I stare at the ceiling; the red Murano chandelier hanging at a weird angle; shadows from the trees creating dancing hands that join the clapping that finally erupts on the other side of my window.

Has he forgotten to hit the disconnect button or does he want me to stay there while he talks to his wife? I stay for a few more seconds and hang up as the clapping subsides.

***

A few days pass, the lockdown is eased, but I am frozen, unable to use my new freedom. I stay inside, as if leaving the shell of my apartment could break the unnatural but now familiar balance.

Alan's final email finds me in this transitional cocoon, sitting on the balcony, trying to finish my last lockdown book. Andrey's ghost is sitting in front of me comfortably, looking at the roofs in silent appreciation, the usual cigarette dangling from his lips. As I scroll through the email, he winks and seems content.

I smile to Andrey and put the book down. My running shoes on, I head outside and start walking towards the river Seine. A heavy golden sun lightens up the evening. I cross half of the bridge, and make my way down onto the narrow island Ile aux Cygnes in the middle of the river. The narrow alley is filled with joggers and dog walkers, all masked. I walk up the stairs of the dreamlike Bir-Hakeim bridge. The trees bordering the alley dance with the wind, as do women's summer dresses, and the grass and wild flowers that have been left to over-grow during lockdown.

I think about Andrey who lost his life defying the system, which he believed to be wrong. I feel proud of my friend but also of Alan as I picture him heading across the Brooklyn Bridge, to do the right thing, as he said in his email. His mask cannot conceal his tears. He halts midway. Battered by the wind coming from all sides, he looks down at the moving water, then takes his phone and calls Chloe.

"I told Cathy everything … and I decided to quit my job." Alan smiles as he talks; he knows that he is doing the right thing again.

IV

Anna

Venice, Italy

Each time Anna's round freckled face appears on my screen, the sound of Venetian bells bursts into my Parisian therapy room. Then we sit together in silence, listening to the loud peals filling our shared virtual space. The blazing Italian sunlight pours into her loft through the open window that I can spot in her background, decorating Anna's hair with a bright halo. The contrast between her pale Slavic features and the colourful Italian surroundings reflects her emigrant condition.

But this time Anna does not wait for the bells' fortissimo to fade out, and breaks her news: "I won't be able to continue my therapy for much longer." Her announcement takes me off guard; we only started a few weeks ago.

Anna's situation in Venice has been precarious from the start, but this time there is no way around it – the end of her doctoral programme means the end of her permit to stay in Europe and of her PhD stipend. She has no hope of getting a job without a visa, or a visa without a job. The home that Anna has made for herself is slipping away from her and returning to her parents' place is not an option.

"I would rather die here," Anna states grimly, a stubborn expression on her close-up face. I know that she means it.

Anna talks about Venice the way other people talk about their romantic partner. "When I first came here I thought I had stepped into my own old dream." She arrived in Venice almost a decade ago to study art and instantly fell in love with the city's crumbling walls that slowly dissolve into the canals' troubled waters. She followed her passion, pursuing a PhD in conservation of architectural heritage. This was a point of no return to Ozersk, her provincial native city in Russia, where there is nothing worth restoring or conserving. By breathing in Venice fully, she expires Ozersk out of her lungs – expelling all the smells, sounds and images of her childhood.

Ozersk is a Soviet settlement in Siberia built around a secret laboratory in the middle of nowhere. Her parents moved there for her father's career as a physicist. They did not put down any roots in this ghost town, where the local soil is frozen for most of the year. Anna always felt out of place there, dreaming about other more welcoming cities, like her mother's native Saint Petersburg, or indeed Venice.

She spells all this out in one long breathless sentence. As she mentions her native town, she averts her eyes, and I can tell that I am losing her to shame. As her story unfolds, the places she describes come alive, but her relationships do not. Her parents struggle to make it to my screen – they remain out of its frame – two ghosts, not malevolent but blurry. For Anna, an only child growing up in an unfriendly foster town, they should have been central to her claustrophobic world.

"What about your parents?" I ask, trying to place her in her relational landscape, but she shrugs in dismissal. It is only when Anna talks about art that her mother comes up – their only connection is their shared passion for art and for Saint Petersburg. Anna discovered as a child the city that her mother has mourned with frustration ever since she had to move to Ozersk. Her mother's job as an art teacher in a provincial school was far from what she had dreamt of during her studies in Saint Petersburg.

"We never talk about important things in my family." The rare Skype conversations that Anna has with her parents make her feel empty and embarrassed. Her mother just sits in front of the camera, motionless and tense. I realise that this is exactly how Anna presents herself on my screen right now.

"And she resents my life in Venice, in the same way she resented my escaping into her art books as a child." Session after session, Anna now talks profusely about her mother's passionate love for Saint Petersburg, paralleling her own attachment for Venice, and I drift away, transported back to the White Nights and the bridges over the canals of Russia's old capital city, where I spent my own childhood. But I can also feel a growing disconnection with her storytelling. Is there something else that she is not telling me? When I ask bluntly, she keeps silent for a moment, looks elsewhere, and her face slowly fades away as she moves sideways, out of my screen's frame.

"I have never been in a romantic relationship," she eventually admits in despair. She has many friends, all creative, free-spirited people, but, now in her mid-thirties, she is desperately single. "My love life is a total disaster!"

As soon as Anna has spilled out this painful truth, the energy is back in our virtual therapy room. It has taken us several sessions to finally reach the real issue. Her love for Venice, as her mother's love for Saint Petersburg, was probably covering up the absence of dependable human attachments.

"My mother has never shown much devotion for anything except for her city, and for art," Anna admits with a sulking child's grimace. She backs away from the camera and nearly disappears into the folds of the old velvet burgundy curtain behind her. On my side of the screen I suddenly feel cold, and notice that she is shivering. She has skilfully recreated a dream place void of intimate relationships for her.

This is where I have to leave her when our hour is over. As we disconnect, I sit in front of my empty screen, acutely feeling Anna's loneliness and despair. Online sessions' endings can feel abrupt. The client is often deprived of a physical transition towards their own reality – no doors to open, no hands to shake, no stairs to climb down. I imagine Anna facing her screen, feeling left on her own, in an uncanny repetition of her childhood experience.

The perspective of Anna losing Venice makes my heart sink. I intuitively grasp the magnitude of her looming loss, having once been an emigrant myself in a precarious situation. The panic in her eyes has awakened the primitive dread of homelessness that I also felt years ago.

***

"I saw on your webpage that you went to art school too" are Anna's first words the next time we meet. My background in art seems to give her hope of a deeper connection with me, one she never fully developed with her mother.

I have to make sure our conversations do not dwell too much on side topics; Anna is very good at steering it that way – avoiding what really matters to her. She may have chosen me as her therapist because of this fortunate parallel in our respective backgrounds, but I want her to understand that I can also care for her, building a reparative experience of bonds that she has lacked. My hope is that our long-distance relationship can become for Anna the safe place that only art or Venice have offered her so far.

This time again, Anna takes the 'art talk' escape route. She tells me in fascinating detail about the church restoration project she is volunteering for. I have to interrupt her: "I suggest we make the most of our limited time today to focus on the subject you brought up during our last session." She freezes on my screen as if I had caught her lying.

"You mentioned the issue of not having a romantic partner ..."

She does not let me finish, visibly relieved by me stepping in: "What's wrong with me? Why can't I give anybody a chance?" Being still single at her age feels shameful to her, a 'chip on her shoulder'.

Sometimes she does end up in her loft with one of the guys she has met at a friend's or at a bar. After sex, the guy would want to stay overnight, offering to make her breakfast the next morning ... but Anna does not let men step into her life.

"I don't enjoy sex very much ... My mind wanders, I day-dream about some painting instead of being in the moment ..."

Anna has actually been playing her arty escape game since childhood. Back then, every time she felt out of her depth with reality, she would slip away, finding refuge in the memory of a painting from her mother's hundreds of art books, full of the promise of a brighter life. Everything that was absent from Anna's grim childhood environment was readily available there, page after page – from the exuberant Dutch still life with its plump fruit and meaty oysters, to the blunt eroticism of Rodin's statues. In her distress, she would seek out art in the same way others would reach out to a friend or to a loving parent.

From those childhood years, Anna keeps a vast imaginary museum, with hundreds of paintings from Dutch and Italian masters, where she can retreat, as her memory brings them back in minute detail. Its vast and warm rooms are always ready to welcome her when it is tough outside. She reminds me of a lonely museum attendant, assigned to look after some windowless basement containing stone-age artefacts that nobody comes to see. When I tell her about it, her eyes turn glassy.

"Where are you now?" I try to bring her back gently.

"Hiding in the bed from the Arnolfini Wedding," she responds with a mischievous smile, as a child who has just been found during a game of hide-and-seek. This painting by Van Eyck is one of the masterpieces from Anna's virtual collection.

She eventually tells me all about her favourite spots to hole up in her beloved paintings – from the cavernous grottos of the Italian Renaissance landscapes to the dark corners of Rembrandt portraits, where she curls up behind the characters' backs, invisible and safe. I am the only person to know her secret hiding spots.

When we hang up and Anna's sad face leaves my screen, I close my eyes, tired by too much screen time, and see a tiny shop, with its hand-painted dusty sign: *'Specchi di Luca'* – Luca's Mirrors. The deep blue walls are covered from floor to ceiling with convex mirrors of all shapes and sizes. I leave my desk and pause in front of one of those mirrors, now hanging on my office wall. I brought back this small piece of my own Venice twenty years ago. It reminds me of the Arnolfini Wedding, just next to the curtain where Anna likes to hide.

As Anna's financial resources become scarce, we meet less often. Our therapy dance takes on a rickety rhythm.

The coronavirus pandemic is already making its deadly way through the north of Italy.

'Venice Carnival cancelled for the first time since the Second World War' I read in the newspaper one morning. I imagine Anna's rollercoaster precarious life taking a new turn with the pandemic.

"How are you coping?" I ask at the start of our next session.

"Not much of an issue, I am naturally socially distant anyway," she shrugs. Her mind goes back to her personal crisis: "Paolo suggests that we get married, it would solve my visa issue." My jaw drops. She never mentioned Paulo before.

Paulo is a set designer and they have worked in the same circles for a few years. He is usually hired with his team to top up the main crew on foreign film productions.

"We are a sort of genius loci, a protective spirit of the place," Paolo likes to joke. "These Americans need us to make sure everything goes smoothly for them here." Paulo and Anna have got drunk together a few times, shared a few pizzas, watched many films in the company of mutual friends, but she never considered him a possible date.

"Why not?"

"I don't know … He is just … too nice. I thought he was gay."

"Is he?"

"I never asked … I just presumed he was. The other day, we were having a drink with the usual suspects, and I mentioned my visa issue. He has no plans to start a family, me neither," Anna sighs, "so he offered to help."

The spirit of Venice, in the shape of Paolo, seems to offer her refuge again. After all, this place has been far more magnanimous to her than people have been.

But his offer, which has a potential of resolving her ongoing visa problem, sends Anna into turmoil. I have to make an enormous effort to hold back and not suggest to her that she accept it. This decision belongs to her.

"What if he eventually falls in love with somebody? I do not want to spoil his chances of marrying that person. I do not want to steal anything from anybody!"

"Why are you talking about stealing?"

"Non lo so, non so cosa fare – I don't know, I don't know what to do," she implores in Italian.

With Anna, we alternate between speaking our native Russian and our shared Italian. We both learned Italian out of rebellion and passion. This mix has become the unique language of her therapy. Switching between the two languages is another way she communicates her emotional states and her thoughts that are not ready to be verbalised yet. This time her choice of Italian informs me about the need for shelter that her mother tongue cannot provide. Anna is panicking.

"Why is he doing this?" Anna's suspiciousness and confusion suggest that being on the receiving end of somebody's generosity is totally foreign to her. What is behind this offer? What does he want from her? Sex? He does not show any romantic interest in her. Money? She is penniless and he knows it.

I tell Anna that she makes me think of a young child who has never been celebrated or offered birthday gifts. When suddenly presented with a beautifully wrapped package, she cries and pushes the unbearable gift away. Receiving what we badly need and never had can be extremely painful as it suddenly brings us back to our endless craving, misery and abandoned hopes.

"This reminds me of something …" Anna looks away and I wait as she sorts out her memories. "At my nursery we were two Annas. One morning, the childminder announced that we would celebrate my birthday. We had a cake; I remember being very excited, as this was the first time I was old enough to blow out my candles." Anna is smiling, but I am already expecting an unpleasant twist to her story. "At the end of that fabulous day, my mother came to collect me, and the truth came out: it was not my birthday, but that of the other Anna. I had basically stolen her celebration and her cake." Three decades later, as Anna tells me this story, her face reddens as she averts her eyes from the screen. "I am still terribly ashamed about that."

Anna has been avoiding gifts ever since that episode and also people who could potentially offer her something she needed.

"Now, each time I hear about a friend's birthday, I feel obliged to bake them a cake." Anna keeps trying to return the gift to the right birthday girl.

"Can I accept such a crazy offer?" she stares at me, imploring for an answer, and I have to resist and avoid screaming a big 'yes'.

"Paolo sounds anything but crazy to me and he is perfectly entitled to make such an offer," I risk. I know very little about this man – can he be trusted?

By the end of the hour I have made up my mind about offering Anna a discounted rate until she finds work and can afford the normal rate again. I secretly hope that my offer will make a difference, help her learn to accept gifts with grace again. When I voice my proposal, her first reaction confirms my hypothesis: "No, I cannot accept this." Anna looks uncomfortable and determined to fight for her right to pay the full fee. "Why should you do this for me?"

"And why not? If I make this offer, I can bear its consequences."

I ask her to take time to think about this and come back to me when she is ready to resume.

***

"Please, could we meet again?" Anna's email reads, a couple of weeks later. "I know I really need this right now and I am grateful for your offer."

***

"I am about to get married." Her puzzled look makes her announcement sound like a question. "I could not tell my parents, they would not understand," she continues.

With Paolo, they went to see his mother. She carefully listened as they explained their agreement; she nodded and congratulated them warmly for the strength of their friendship.

"I have not even considered him as a close friend ... and here I was sitting in his mother's house, eating the pasta she had prepared for me, chatting with them both as if ..." Anna is overwhelmed. The warmth of Paolo's home, his mother accepting her son's decision without questioning it (or at least not in front of her), such a contrast with her own parents. "My mother would have made a fuss about it. I am sure she would insist that a sham marriage was some kind of trap ..." She certainly knew about traps, having followed her husband to a ghost town and given up on her career in the arts.

Paolo's mother is from a small town near Venice; their roots are deeply and securely planted in the local humid soil. So unlike hers. Realising this, Anna is torn apart, both wanting to get closer to this welcoming home, but also feeling compelled to run away as far and fast she can.

"As we parted in front of Paolo's mother's house, to go to our separate ways, I felt a bizarre pang of regret."

She knew little or nothing about his life outside of the friendly moments they had shared so far, never alone, always surrounded by the chatty company of their group of mutual friends.

She had stood in the middle of the street for a minute, watching his thin silhouette walk away, lightly – his head high and his movements relaxed – as a very secure person. Paolo would have no problem with accepting a surprise gift, she thought out of the blue, and for a second she wants to bake him a cake and stand at his side as he blows out the candles ...

***

It has been a few weeks since our last conversation. I receive a short note from Anna in an out-of-breath Italian: "Sposata davvero. Che strano – Officially married. How weird."

I write back congratulating her on her gracious acceptance of Paolo's friendly gift and for her new right to stay forever in Italy. "I can finally breathe freely again," she responds. I exhale with relief.

***

The pandemic is developing exponentially. The week after their marriage, lockdown is imposed in Italy and Anna reaches out urgently: "Please, could we meet this week?" It is already Thursday evening. Anna rarely asks for anything directly, so I make sure we can meet quickly.

"I could not imagine this happening …" Anna looks baffled, as she connects to our session from an unusual place, Paolo's home.

They now must spend lockdown in the same place together. The administration representatives will visit Paolo's apartment unannounced in order to check that the marriage is genuine. Paolo cannot pretend that Anna happens to be out as this is now forbidden.

Luckily, Paolo's flatmate has left town to spend lockdown somewhere else, so Anna will temporarily use his vacant bedroom.

The reality of sharing a roof has fallen down on them, and I am secretly glad that Anna cannot retreat. Her mother showed love for distant and unattainable objects, but made no effort to return to Saint Petersburg, silently accepting her loveless life in Ozersk. Could this explain why Anna chose a distant therapist? Was it a more acceptable risk because I live hundreds of miles away? When she leaves my screen, I am just hoping that Paolo is the decent man he seems to be.

***

At the next session, Anna looks jumpy but unhurt. "He makes me breakfast." She pauses ... "It is actually delicious, with fresh moka and everything," she smiles, relaxing a little. Paolo is the first man that she cannot simply oust before dawn, because, in this instance, the place is his; and they are stuck there. I start envisioning more therapeutic opportunities with this unexpected turn of events.

She shows me the windowless bedroom where she is temporarily spending most of her days. It is surprisingly spacious but this can hardly compensate for the absence of daylight.

These first days of living at Paolo's place have not been easy for Anna. The strict lockdown order has somehow turned them into inmates. All Paolo's film gigs are put on indefinite hold and, sociable as he is, he struggles to adapt to this new loss of freedom.

"I feel like such a nuisance. Invading his space was not part of the deal," she pleads.

"Does he complain about it?"

"No, he does not. He seems content not to be alone ... as if nothing strange was happening, as if this terrible plague was not at our door."

Anna has never lived with anybody before, except for her parents and a few passing flatmates. As a child, she spent a lot of time in her room, reading and drawing endless imaginary landscapes of places she had never seen. As a teenager she would barely leave her bedroom. Her parents never even knocked on her door; her room soon became a solitary space of confinement.

As we talk, a huge black cat appears in the background and settles on the bedhead, as still as an Egyptian statue, and turns his round, yellow eyes directly at Anna's neck.

"Meet Laura ... I think this cat is suspicious of me."

Paolo picked her up as a tiny kitten fifteen years ago. They have been inseparable ever since. "Sometimes I am afraid she may attack me from behind."

"Have you tried making friends with her?"

"No way. We keep our distance."

"I am not interested in stealing YOUR Paolo," she turns to the stationary cat.

Venice, the same as Paris, is now empty; the tourists are gone and the shops are closed indefinitely. After a few weeks, Anna and Paolo settle into a strange marital life, imposed by the lockdown and the awaited visit from the authorities. They take turns to shop for groceries – the only short daily outings that are now allowed; he likes cooking; she does not mind cleaning. All goes strangely smoothly.

"We barely go out and survive on pasta and eggs ... I am getting used to this room. Yesterday I ventured out to top up our coffee supplies". She tells me nostalgically about passing her favourite places, all shut and deserted. Only one of them, the craftsman mirror shop, was open. As she went past it, the owner, Luca, was taking the mirrors off the window, preparing for the long closure. After making sure the street was empty, he let her in and closed the shutters. They shared an unauthorised coffee, standing in the shop, at a distance. "How sad, it feels like the plague is back in Venice," he commented.

"He told me about another Russian girl who bought a mirror from him twenty years ago and they eventually became friends ... He was secretly in love with her ... I think this is why Luca likes me." I learn something about my past, a gift that Anna has unknowingly smuggled for me, an ironic turn in this therapy.

We are all somehow connected – Anna, Luca, me, Venice, Van Dyck and even the Arnolfini spouses ...

***

"We watched a film together … This time it almost felt like a date."

Anna blushes as she tells me how some of their friends, aware of their arrangement, mock them as *'sposini'* – newly-weds.

In contrast, Paolo seems unperturbed and smiles silently in response. Anna is generally confused about the meaning of him smiling so easily – is he mocking her? Or is he genuinely happy?

Her parents gave away so little about their emotional lives that Anna finds it hard to read facial expressions and to work out other people's emotions if they have not been clearly verbalised.

"Imagining you as a little girl always alone in your room makes me feel sad," I share with Anna.

She hides her eyes again, visibly shaken by the impact of so much emotion shared. She admits she finds it hard to look at my face on her screen. It is 'too open'. The online nature of our sessions imposes a close-up; Anna can barely avoid reading my emotional reactions to her words. I hope that this exposure will help her become more comfortable with other people's emotions, especially Paolo's.

***

"Why am I so down?" Anna wonders. The nicer Paolo is to her, the more she spirals down into a dark place of sorrow. His caring presence, which is only temporary, reveals what Anna has missed so badly in her childhood, and will miss again when this pretence is over.

Several weeks into their 'perfect marriage' play, the authorities have still not showed up. Anna's anxiety is growing. Did they forget about them? With the lockdown, the administration apparatus has come to a halt, leaving many in limbo.

"If tomorrow you could return to your room and resume your life, how would you feel?" Anna looks away, visibly torn.

"Relieved, I guess …" As I wait silently for more, she continues, "but also a little sad." Anna is starting to like Paolo's constant presence, but it is far too risky to put this realisation into words yet.

"It was my birthday last week," Anna announces matter-of-factly.

"You did not mention it last time …"

"No, I did not. I hate my birthday. And with lockdown I was freed from doing anything about it."

"So you did not have to bake a cake to treat everybody else for your birthday?"

"No, I did not … but Paolo did." Saying this, Anna looks embarrassed.

"How was it?"

"Absolutely inedible," she laughs.

"I am not talking about the cake, but about you. How did you feel about him surprising you with a cake?"

"Terrible. I escaped to my room and cried for an hour. Now he will really think that I am a complete mess."

Paolo remained calm. He stayed in the kitchen, washing the dishes and waited for Anna to re-emerge. When she did not, he finally knocked on her door. She tells me about this moment in bewilderment.

"He asked why I was upset, whether he had done something wrong, whether I hated cakes. So I told him my nursery cake story."

He reassured her that she was the only girl named Anna that he had known so far. They ended up blowing out the candles together and feeding the disgusting cake to the seagulls. Then they watched a film and parted to their respective rooms just before midnight.

"He didn't even try to kiss me."

"Did you want him to?"

"Yes, but just for a second …" In response to a smile that I cannot hide, Anna smiles herself. She is ready to give Paolo a chance and I am starting to like the man.

"Do you think I should trust him?"

Of course I cannot answer this; it is for Anna to decide. But clearly I would like her to take this risk and give the relationship a chance.

***

When I see Anna again, connecting from bed, she looks frozen, and all the bubbly energy that was there in the previous session has dissipated.

"I want to leave this place."

"What happened?" My heart sinks as I imagine the worse.

"Paolo's old girlfriend turned up. They went out for a walk." She delivers the news in a robotic way, all emotion drained out of her face. "She doesn't care less about the lockdown."

Paolo's cat jumps on Anna's bed, her tail brushes the screen. Anna automatically strokes the cat, and she moves onto her lap to comfortably curl up.

"I see that you made peace with Laura."

"His ex-girlfriend's name is Laura. He actually adopted the kitten when she left him." Anna strokes the cat's black fur in an automatic movement but the look on her face is murderous.

"Did he not mention her before?"

"No. He told me today, as she was already on her way. She came back from Rome, her father has just died from Covid."

We both feel deflated by Laura-the-girl's return.

"You could have warned me, I was starting to buy into this fairy-tale," Anna tells the cat what she is too embarrassed to tell me.

"Why do you think Paolo had not told you about Laura, I mean the girl …?"

"Maybe because I never asked? I was too afraid to show him that I cared."

"So, he has no idea that you actually like him?"

"No." Saying this, Anna lowers her head towards the cat and avoids looking into the camera.

"But you do?" Anna does not need to respond, as we both know the answer. She nods silently.

Then I hear the distant noise of a door opening, and two voices talking loudly behind the door. Laura the cat jumps down from Anna's lap and runs to the door to greet her owner. Anna is in a panic. She looks around frantically, in search of a hiding spot. She has no time to retreat as we hear a knock on the door, and Paolo's voice calls her name: "Anna, scusa, sei occupata? Ti volevo presentare Laura – Anna, sorry, are you busy? I would like to introduce Laura to you."

"I have no choice, I guess" Anna whispers and I nod in approval. I have to resist wishing her luck before we hang up.

As after watching a particularly gripping episode of a TV series, I have to wait until the following week to learn what Laura is like. In the meantime I worry about the impact her sudden appearance will have on Anna's life.

"I actually liked Laura a lot. She is clever and bold." Their relationship with Paolo is well in the past. But Paolo, with his usual disarming honesty, also confirmed that Laura was probably interested in resuming where they had left it a few years ago, when she moved to Rome.

"And what about you?" Anna surprised herself by daring to ask Paolo.

"I am not," he responded, looking her in the eyes with a smile that Anna decoded as 'flirty'. She was definitely making progress in reading Paolo's emotional signals.

This is where they left it for the night, which was sleepless for Anna, who kept thinking about Paolo. She did not dare to join him in his room; he did not knock on hers either. This time, she was hoping he would and stayed in bed, restless, listening to the night silence hoping to hear the light steps of his bare feet in the corridor. With Laura's unexpected entrance, her fear of losing Paolo made it to the surface, impossible to ignore any more.

***

"Laura called me." Anna surprises me at the next session. "She has an aunt who works at the town hall. She had rung her to enquire about our situation. The woman was able to access our file and we do not have to worry about the visit anymore …"

What a clever bitch, I cannot avoid thinking to myself.

"Does Paolo know about this?" I ask, unable to mask my irritation with Laura.

"No, but I have to tell him, don't I?" Anna implores me to take this responsibility from her, which is not for me to do. Her face is animated. This is probably the first time I see her anger coming to the surface with such clarity and strength. Her usually pale cheeks redden and her green eyes sparkle.

I have to handle two opposite emotions myself – I am angry at Laura's Machiavellian move, but, simultaneously, the therapist in me is excited about the therapeutic potential of the disappointment that Anna is going through. Is she finally ready to take ownership of her feelings for Paolo and fight for their relationship?

As I write my notes after the session, I am still irritated with Paolo's ex-girlfriend. Anna was making such progress in trusting Paolo who was turning into my unexpected therapy ally. I was starting to believe in her fairy-tale myself. When my anger eventually fades, I surrender to the sobering reality; it was a sham marriage after all.

At least, in accepting Paolo's gift, Anna has acquired a new and essential emotional experience. Even if she has to resume her lonely existence, she has learnt that she can entrust a person with her love – not an artwork or a town. This particular gift from Paolo was really for her.

***

I only see Anna a few weeks later. The old burgundy curtain is in the background, she is back in her flat and looks miserable.

"Here I am again."

We stay in silence listening to the bells' crescendo that welcomes us back to our virtual therapy room. I watch Anna slowly returning to her familiar emotional space. She is terribly lonely again, with little hope that anybody will knock on her door. With the extended lockdown, she has no restoration work to go to; her flatmates have all left Venice to spend lockdown at their parents; and her marital bubble has come to an abrupt end.

"I could not face him, I would probably have burst into tears, and made a complete fool of myself. So I just left a note and went."

"How did he react?"

"He has been trying to call, but I am not answering."

I realise that Anna has not left her room for three days. She has mostly stayed in bed, too ashamed of her renewed loneliness to re-engage with the world.

"Laura always gets what she wants," Anna says, and I can only agree. That girl was surely luckier in her childhood; she developed an impressive confidence. Laura's Venice is real. Anna is left to her books and to her imaginary hiding games, to her empty museum rooms, in which nobody ever looks for her.

"Anna, I am here, don't slip away." I see her retreating to her safe imaginary heavens. She nods, tears in her eyes. "And what do *you* want?" I ask bluntly, hoping to stop her downward spiral. She looks confused, but I wait in silence, not letting her off the hook.

"To be with Paolo," she admits finally in a tiny, barely audible voice.

"Could you say that more loudly please?"

She repeats it and this time I can hear her clearly. She now sounds assertive and owns her feelings for Paolo.

"Maybe I should tell him about it." This time it is not a question, but a statement. I nod; proud of her newly found voice. Anna seems impatient – or maybe scared of losing her fragile strength.

She finally picks up her phone. "Can I?" I nod, breaking all boundary rules, and she starts typing her text message for Paolo.

When she is done, she puts the phone away and looks at me. Her face is alive with all the emotions she has been keeping inside. Her phone beeps only a few seconds later – a symbolic knock on her door, and she grabs it to read his response.

On my screen, I watch her face transforming further.

"He's invited me for dinner at his place tonight ..." Anna's face lights up, and I smile in response, bewildered. This time Anna does not need to retreat to her imaginary museum.

Paolo has turned up at her hiding spot to find her. And this time, she is ready to be found.

V

JP

Brussels, Belgium

"I have put myself in a terrible, terrible situation," his anxious but melodious voice sounds slightly exotic, with its Belgian accent.

Agatha Christie's Poirot comes readily to my mind – a quaint little man with an egg-shaped head and a stiff moustache. This is the first time I have met with JP and I know nothing about him yet. His initial email briefly stated that he needed therapy and that it was urgent.

The slow to emerge image feeds my curiosity, as I wait for his face to appear in the Zoom frame.

"I don't know where to start … I have never done this before," JP continues almost without breathing, as I stare at my still empty screen.

"Maybe you could start by switching on your camera so that we can meet each other properly?"

"Do I have to do this?" JP's voice loses its Poirot-esque notes, as his restraint gives way to extreme anxiety.

Of course he does. My own camera has been dutifully on and my own lonely face is flickering in the corner of an otherwise blank window. I start feeling exposed and uncomfortable myself.

"It would be preferable and your therapy would benefit from us getting to know each other better." I have to take a deep breath. My reserve of patience is running low, worn out by the lockdown.

He keeps silent for a long moment, struggling to make up his mind. My imagination is running wild – what does he have to hide? A horribly scarred face? The messy room of a hoarder? I picture him playing nervously with his computer mouse, breathing heavily … I can almost hear him sweating …

"I know this may be difficult for you so, please, take your time," I try to reassure him (or myself), uncertain whether I still want to see what he has to hide.

After some more breathing and fidgeting from JP, my screen finally comes to life. His face makes its delayed entrance into my Parisian office: average features, well groomed, grey tortured eyes behind some heavily framed designer spectacles. Rather disappointing for my fevered imagination. No apparent reasons for hiding.

He attempts a contorted smile as his transparent eyes are screaming for help. The room from where he connects is dim, and I can barely distinguish in the background a large library filled with thick volumes. The yellow light coming from an invisible desk lamp gives the shape of a macabre mask to JP's face.

"This is very uncomfortable," he volunteers eventually.

"Uncomfortable? In what way?" I am impatient to make a proper start.

"You will think I am a sick person."

"I promise to honestly tell you what I think, but before I can do that I have to hear your story."

He exhales loudly.

"Please, tell me a little about yourself. Where are you right now?"

"In Brussels. This is my gallery. I deal in primitive arts, African art mostly." He moves back from the screen letting me see the background – two impressive masks hang on the wall, reigning over his desk and probably over the whole room.

"They come from my father's collection," JP sounds proud.

"Was he in the art business too?"

"Yes, he was the one who started this gallery. He was a very respected man. He passed away twenty years ago."

"What kind of person was he?" As soon as I ask, his face transforms – an instant change of masks – now JP looks irritated.

"I am not here to talk about my father!" he snaps.

Usually, this kind of statement indicates quite the opposite. I can almost see his father's ghost grinning at me from behind JP's back. Like all therapists, I am used to confronting other people's parents; their ghosts do not impress me anymore.

"What would you like to talk about instead?"

"I do not know if I should talk at all, what's the point anyway?" With the air leaving his lungs, JP suddenly looks like a deflating balloon.

"Would you like to tell me about your 'terrible situation'?" I push again.

JP's eyes shout 'no' but he nods in despair, nearly out of breath again. "I guess I have no choice. My apartment is right above the gallery. With the current lockdown, my business has moved online, and I work down here most evenings dealing with my clients' enquiries and orders." Every word seems to cause him pain and I'm following every movement of his lips. "A few days ago I was sitting right here, at my desk …" He stops, unable to go any further. His shame is almost palpable, and I feel for him. It would be so easy to let him off the hook, postponing his confession, but we have to push through, to let the painful truth out. JP is silent now, with his face buried in his hands, he seems to weep silently. As much as I want to free him from this torture, I cannot, not until he lets it out.

"This is just too difficult."

"Would it be easier to tell me about it with your camera off?"

"Yes, please," he implores, his face promptly leaving my screen. "I have a son who is fifteen. Charles is a very delicate and sensitive boy." His voice is reduced to a whisper, filled with so much tenderness that I would forgive him whatever terrible thing he has done. "So that day he came downstairs … sometimes he has these terrible nightmares … and I … I was talking with one of the girls." JP stops, his breathing getting heavier again. I have to let him know that I am still here, to avoid his confession becoming a monologue. To take responsibility for his actions, JP needs a witness.

"One of the girls?" I ask to keep him going.

"Webcam girls." JP finally bursts the bubble of his shame. "I've never met any of them. They are just … images on my screen."

Somehow like me, I cannot help noticing.

Once the disgraceful truth has been voiced, JP cannot stop. He tells me the rest of the story in one long breathless tirade.

'His ruin' started a year ago, as he stumbled across an article about the webcam girls industry, and its mostly Eastern European women in need of fast money. As he keeps talking, I am silently wondering whether he knows where I grew up.

The very first time, he thought he would just try once. But soon he was spending hours, locked in his office, watching women performing for him in front of their cameras. Since then JP has been meeting with them online every week, sometimes several nights in a row. Everything was under control, he was very careful in covering his tracks until that unfortunate evening, when his son had a nightmare and came down to find him in the gallery.

"Could you switch your camera back on?"

To establish real contact and for JP to face his shame, I need him on my screen. After all, with the webcam girls, the porn addict is accustomed to discharging his inner turmoil and semen without the risk of developing intimacy. But to help JP out of his drama, we will need to develop a proper therapeutic relationship, turning the flimsy online connection into a proper *connection*.

There is no immediate answer to my request, and I wonder whether JP is still there, when his image comes back to my screen.

"You must think I am a terrible person," he states grimly.

"Doing something that you find terrible does not make you a terrible person."

He looks at me with desperate hope. "I do not know why I am doing this. I love my family. I treasure my son. And now I risk destroying it all with my reckless behaviour. This is so stupid!"

"Is it? Can you think of any reason for this?"

"A reason? There is no other bloody reason than my being a self-indulging pig!" JP sounds suddenly angry. "I am just like my father!" he mumbles, hiding his face in disgust.

"What do you mean?"

"Nothing, forget about it. I told you that I don't want to talk about my father."

Now I am furious and my heart is racing. It takes me a few deep breaths to not lash out at JP. "Stop being such a coward!" I want to scream at him, but luckily I bite my tongue in time. The strength of my emotional reaction takes me by surprise; in front of me, JP is genuinely struggling with shame and regret. He is very skilled at pushing me away when he is distressed, although I am the person supposed to be helping him. Is it something he does outside of therapy as well, with his significant others? When I ask, JP shrugs. "I have no idea."

His relationship with his wife Louise has always been a good one, never any conflict. They share the same passion for primitive arts. Louise works at the gallery too, and their family business has been flourishing against all odds. How did she handle the news about his virtual affairs?

"She does not know about it," JP admits. Their son Charles, too scared of the repercussions this could have on the family, has been adamant that his father keep it secret. In telling me this, JP can hardly conceal his relief. "I know it is not fair on my son, but I could not refuse him this, he was absolutely hysterical."

We play this cat-and-mouse game for the rest of the hour. I keep trying to understand what kind of emotional distress lies behind his webcam girls habit, and JP stubbornly resists any direct disclosure. "I don't understand what you want from me!" The more I push, the more defensive he gets. When our time is over, I give up reluctantly.

By the end of the session we both feel exhausted and ready to part.

"I will let you know about the next time," he drops as a goodbye, and I doubt I will ever see him again. When he disconnects, I can nearly hear the bang of a slammed door.

"My son isn't well, can we talk again?" JP writes in a hurried email a few days later.

This time, his camera is on from the start. His pale face is flanked by the masks on the wall behind.

"No hiding today?" I ask.

"No. I am fed up with all this sneaking around!"

The thought of his own son catching him at his computer, 'messing around' with some plump redhead, keeps haunting JP. Since the disgraceful incident, Charles' insomnia has got worse. He is unable to get rid of the image of his father masturbating in front of a webcam girl. The scene is firmly imprinted on his retina, and his brain is stuck on this 'dirty stuff'. I would like to reassure JP that he has not damaged his son in any irreparable way, but I just cannot. Most probably the boy will not forget what he saw, and JP's relationship with Charles will never go back to what it was. This is a hard truth, but JP has to accept it.

"Have I messed it all up?" JP implores, and I nod, hoping to look compassionate.

JP's face crumbles; he jumps up and leaves his desk. As he disappears from my screen, the masks are looking at me from their wall. I do not know where he has gone; only a distant door slamming indicates that he has left the room. This is the first time I can study the masks in detail – one has a round face flanked with a jagged aureole, which makes it look like a scary sun; another is a hellish accumulation of different parts of animals, all mashed up together, as from some painting by Bosch. I suddenly get goose bumps.

"Sorry." JP is wiping his mouth and looks even paler than usual. "I was sick … You surely find me disgusting. I am sorry you have to see this."

I do not find him disgusting; now that his struggle has been exposed, all my earlier irritation is gone and I feel for him.

"Why did I not lock that bloody door?" Usually, when JP retreats to the gallery to work late at night, he carefully closes the door behind him. But this time he left it unlocked. This faux pas seems to preoccupy him more than any deeper question behind his self-destructive behaviour.

"Let's try to understand why you felt the urge to seek out the virtual girls despite your love for your family."

"It is all this lockdown … It is driving me mad."

It would be easy to echo his words; the sudden lack of freedom has been a maddening experience for many (including me), but this would be a much too easy way out for JP. I am starting to understand that he often looks for an escape route, avoiding any situation that he finds emotionally challenging or uncomfortable.

"What is it exactly about the lockdown that you are finding difficult?"

"I don't know … seeing my son stuck in the house … He wanders around, looking lonely."

Being stuck at home can certainly be hard on a teenager. I think about my own daughter, roughly Charles's age, spending hours watching movies, chatting with her friends, always on her phone.

"Have you ever asked your son whether he felt lonely?"

"No, I have not … I just presumed …"

So, there is a lot of guessing going on. Could JP be feeling lonely himself? After all, it is not unusual to project our own unconscious or untold emotional experience onto our children. And JP, with his tendency to hide, must be good at accumulating untold experiences …

"How was it for *you* to be fifteen?"

JP looks at me startled: "Why do you ask?" His shooting back a question at me instead of responding confirms that we may be onto something. The rest of the conversation feels like I am pushing a closed door that JP is holding from the other side with all his weight.

After some elaborate back and forth, we agree that he would ask his son how he has been feeling during the lockdown. Despite his love for Charles, JP acknowledges that they rarely talk about feelings in their family, and he knows little about what is really going on in his son's blonde head.

"He is a quiet boy, rather introverted, just like myself." I secretly hope that by talking more with his son, we may not only challenge his projection, but also help the adolescent work through the difficult feelings caused by his father's reckless behaviour.

As we close our session, I feel exhausted. JP is not ready to let me into his past, safely locked behind that door. My head is hurting mildly, probably the consequence of all this door banging.

∗∗∗

"I talked with my son." JP starts the next session vehemently.

His strange tone soon has an explanation – my intuition was right; Charles was actually 'cool' with staying at home. He has been mastering a new video game with his online friends. JP looks simultaneously relieved and defensive.

"And what about you? How have you been feeling during these months?"

"Not so different from the usual," JP responds stubbornly, but he avoids looking at the screen. He takes his glasses off for the first time and rubs his eyes. He looks young and strangely vulnerable.

"Are you telling me that you have been feeling lonely for a long time?"

"I suppose so …"

It turns out JP was painfully lonely all through his childhood. He was not close to his father, who was a loner, keeping his work and his passions away from his family. His mother was depressed and she was eventually admitted to a mental health institution. Once a month they would visit her on the psychiatric ward. JP was scared by these visits. His mother was officially 'mad'; her distracted and dishevelled appearance confirmed this diagnosis. JP felt that her bubble was impenetrable to him, and did not want to see her in this state. By the time he turned fourteen, these visits stopped abruptly. She had managed to kill herself, by stepping out of the clinic's window. Only much later did JP learn the true circumstances of her death. His father never remarried, and only grew more obsessed with his African art collection and business.

JP tells me about his father's habit of locking himself in his office every night. As a child he had a lot of dreams and fantasies about what his father may have been doing behind that door, in that room where JP was not allowed.

He still remembers his French nanny reading him to sleep to the 'Barbe Bleue' – Bluebeard – fairy tale. He lay in bed, terrified and fascinated by the story, and probably relating to the young wife's desire to enter the secret room. The heavy wooden door to his father's office often appeared in his childhood dreams. Sometimes it led to an enchanted world, sometimes to some scary, nightmarish universe. In one instance he remembered seeing blood coming from underneath the door, staining the thick beige carpet, and eventually flooding their house.

Why had his mother become mad? He still remembered the sound of her laughing and playing the piano. She clearly was not mad back then. Did it have something to do with his father's office? As a little boy, JP came up with many scary explanations for her illness and somehow it would always go back to that locked room.

His father never talked about his wife's mental illness and JP never dared to ask.

When he turned twelve, JP was sent to a boys' boarding school. This allowed his father to travel to Africa in search of new, unexplored tribes and bring back tribal artwork. During the holidays back home, JP would discover his father's trophies from his expeditions. He was fascinated by these strange objects, which eventually became the only meaningful thing his father shared with him.

"How did you end up becoming an art dealer yourself?"

"I never planned to … it just happened. When my father died

JP

he left me his collection, including these masks … They are actually worth a lot of money."

"But you have not sold them …"

"No …" JP turns around to face the masks, and I watch the back of his head while he is scrutinising them in silence. After a few long moments, when he finally turns back to the screen, his eyes are wet.

"What do they mean to you?"

"They have always been there … hanging on his office wall."

The masks were allowed where JP was not; this made them silent witnesses of whatever his father was doing behind that door. As a little boy he was scared of the masks. His mother disliked them too. She never wanted them anywhere around the house.

"So, have you eventually figured out what was going on behind the closed door of your father's office?"

"No, not really … He was clearly not surfing the web …" The mystery of the locked door, central to his childhood, remains unresolved.

"What is your best adult guess?"

"He may have been escaping my mother's illness, and he did not know how to handle me …"

JP's father died having named his friend Paul, his business partner and co-owner of the gallery, as the executor of his will. Paul sorted through the collection, making an inventory and selling some less valuable objects. JP was only seventeen and was sent back to school promptly after the funeral.

When JP came back to Brussels at the end of the school year, Paul had rented out the gallery. With the money he had inherited, JP went to travel the world for a gap year. What remained of his father's collection was stored in the cellar of the family house.

"At that point I just felt I had to go …" With no close family left in Brussels, no special attachment to the family house, which remained unoccupied, leaving the country was liberating.

JP worked for a few years as a junior travel agent in Kinshasa, the capital of the former Belgian Congo. One day he received a call from Paul's wife. Paul had died.

"For some reason I felt terribly sad, something I do not remember feeling after my father's passing ..."

With Paul's death, JP's hopes of entering his father's secret world were fading. His father's metaphorical office door now shut in his face with a definite bang.

JP returned to Brussels to take care of his estate. He rediscovered his city, the Petit Sablon area of the old town. A few months later, JP had settled down in the family house and restored the ground floor space, where he opened his own primitive arts gallery.

"This very place." JP makes a gesture, pointing to the sombre bookcases and the masks.

"Have you ever tried to speak to people who were close to your parents?"

"With her mental issues and stay in an asylum, my mother ended up without any friends. My father ... as I mentioned, he was a very reserved man. Apart from his partner Paul ..."

"And Paul died before you could really talk to him, right?"

JP nods, and I am unsure whether his facial expression shows disappointment or relief.

"Did he have a family?"

Actually he did. JP had briefly met Paul's wife Françoise at his funeral. They had exchanged Christmas cards ever since, although no more than that. She lived in Uccle, a chic suburb just south of Brussels.

"Do you think she may know something about your father's life?"

"She may well …" As JP responds, his eyes slide away from the camera. "I have never really tried to pay a visit, and anyway now with the lockdown orders, I could not even go there".

"Why haven't you tried to find out more about your father?"

My question leads to a long silence. JP looks confused, unsure. I want to give him time to reflect on the question, although I think I already know the answer. We sit in silence for some time, before JP's voice finally makes it to the surface.

"I am not sure I want to know …"

Behind his father's locked door, JP is terrified of finding something horrible, something that he would not be able to handle. But this avoidance comes with a high cost. His unconscious tendency to repeat his father's parenting style, his self-isolating in his work, and especially his recent re-enacting of the 'secret room' drama with the webcam girls are threatening to destroy his family.

I suddenly realise that, as I sit in front of my screen listening to JP, I feel an acute curiosity about JP's father's office. If I was free of professional ethical considerations, I would have looked up Françoise's details and called her. The curiosity that JP has buried for years under his fear is now growing stronger in me. I tell JP how I feel and his face comes back to life.

"I know the feeling!"

As the young JP was standing in the dark in front of that door, his heart was beating heavily, and he was swept by a wave of excitement. He was supposed to stay in bed. Had his nanny or his father found out that he was breaking the rules, he would have been harshly scolded. Imagining his father arriving at an undiscovered African village, led there by a guide, added to his excitement. JP was never allowed to travel with his father. Only after his death did he discover the African continent.

"I outdid my father in terms of exploring Africa. I travelled further than he ever did," JP tells me with a faint smile. JP's curiosity for his father's remote world had actually turned into an obsession.

More recently, each time he connected with a webcam girl, he felt a wave of excitement that reminded him of his childhood. Doing something forbidden was exhilarating, but also triggered the fear of being discovered; the same set of contradictory emotions that he felt as a boy in front of his father's locked room.

He had never found the courage to push open that door; immobilised by the fear of punishment, he had just stood there, frozen and excited by the pictures he could imagine – fantasies of masked African dancers, of young naked women performing mysterious rituals around the fire.

Now with the webcam girls, he was somehow re-enacting that old situation, a mysterious webcam girl was somewhere behind a door, and hitting the 'call' button on his computer would make her appear. He would then step into the forbidden space – something he had not done during his childhood.

"And what about your son? Do you ever let Charles into your office and into your life?"

"Not much, I suppose."

"Just like your father …?"

JP nods. His face is overtaken by a wave of pain as he realises this.

"Maybe it is time to let him in?"

"Do you mean into my office?"

"Yes, into the office as well …" Charles has to learn that his father is doing other things in his gallery, not just watching webcam girls.

"But he is not interested in the arts, not at all." As I hear JP, I imagine the exact same defensive and condescending tone of his father's.

"Have you tried to share your passion with him?"

"Maybe I haven't tried enough," he acknowledges grimly.

A loud knock on the door makes JP panic. "It could be Charles! What do I do?"

I have no time to respond, as the banging gets louder.

"Papa!" I can hear the teenager's high-pitched voice; he sounds hysterical.

"J'arrive – Coming," shouts JP towards the door, and then whispers into the microphone. "Can I introduce you to him? Please? Otherwise he will think I am talking to one of those girls again …"

I acquiesce, without much thought. As JP leaves my screen to unlock the door, all kind of considerations are rushing through my mind – what should I make of this unexpected chat with the boy? How can I use this surprising opportunity for JP's therapeutic benefit? I have no time to sort through this storm as Charles breaks into my computer screen. As the father introduces me somehow pompously as his 'doctor', he stares at me in bewilderment. I guess he was not expecting the woman on the screen to be dressed.

"Does she even speak French?" he asks defiantly.

"Charles, please, don't be rude. Anastasia is my doctor."

I greet the boy as if it was in my own office: "Would you like to take a seat?" JP moves another chair towards the desk and sits down. He is trying to collaborate.

"Charles, I know this has not been an easy time for you," I start tentatively, and he frowns. His face still has a babyish shape. With his blonde curls, he looks angelic. When he finally looks at the screen, his blue eyes show pain that is far from childish.

"I am fine," he drops with disdain for the adults' decadent world.

"Your father is worried about you, he told me about your sleeping difficulties …"

"I am fine," he insists but keeps looking away.

Charles stubbornly guarding his defences, as his father did at the beginning of our work. Now JP is just sitting there letting me do the talking; his pale face is hopeful though.

"Charles, I am so sorry …" JP's voice is filled with shame and regret.

His son does not move; he seems immobilised by all the confusing feelings boiling inside. I feel for them both.

"Charles, is there anything that you would like to tell your father?"

His head moves in an almost invisible nod.

"I love you, even after this …" he murmurs without looking at either of us.

I can see that JP is now crying silently, without moving. He stares at me, his face contorted. "Hug your son, for God's sake," I want to scream. Do I have to spell it out to him? Finally he reaches out to Charles awkwardly, and they both weep silently, like two real men.

We end the session in this rather melodramatic manner, and I leave them together in an embrace that will hopefully start a new chapter in their relationship. I let my screen go blank and leave the notes for the next day. I realise that I am really missing my daughter, who is waiting for me on the other side of my locked office door …

***

The next time we meet, JP is shaken after a vivid dream from the night before. He visibly struggles with the camera lens again, so we switch it off. This has now become a trick that we use to help him regulate his exposure and shame. As soon as his face disappears from my screen, his voice gets steadier. I close my eyes and listen to its now familiar music, letting it guide me through his dream.

JP is trapped in a long, empty corridor, which has multiple

doors; he does not know which one he is supposed to open. He is looking for something important without knowing what it is. All doors look identical – plain white doors firmly shut. After some wandering, he discovers one door that looks different: its heavily carved wooden frame is exactly the same as the one that led to his father's office. JP pushes it and steps into the room. But it is my office, not his father's. I am smiling to him invitingly and start undressing, just like the webcam girls would do.

As I keep my eyes closed, I live the uncanny experience of being simultaneously in two different places. I understand why JP has had to switch off his camera. The dream version of me, I learn, ends up performing an erotic dance, and the masks leave their wall to join in.

It takes JP a few minutes to switch the camera back on. He is visibly embarrassed, but we both realise how meaningful this dream is. I am glad that he is able to share it; this reveals how much progress we have made in forging trust.

"What do you make of it?"

"I do not know. It is so embarrassing. You are nothing like those girls."

I reassure JP that I am sure about the differences indeed, but what about his father's door leading to my office, a room that he has never visited in reality?

"Maybe by coming here, I can finally understand …"

By pushing my virtual door, he hopes to finally penetrate his father's secret space. The timing of the dream, just after his son joined us for the session, is probably not by chance. By welcoming Charles into our shared virtual space, I have shown JP an example of how this can be done.

Are there other doors that remain closed to him?

"Well maybe I should talk about my wife."

For a few years she has developed a passion for mindfulness; since then she often retreats into her 'meditation corner' and disappears into her own world. She is often out of bed early to 'meditate', even missing breakfast.

"It is actually her therapist who got her hooked on this whole meditation thing," JP remarks reproachfully, as if I should carry the responsibility for all other shrinks out there.

"Do you miss her being closer to you?"

JP shrugs in his usual dismissive way, but now I have learnt to pick up on his subtler signals – he takes his glasses off and looks away from the screen.

"I don't even know any more what 'close to her' means," he admits.

They felt like accomplices at the very beginning of their relationship, when they travelled to Africa together, following African merchants to remote villages, hunting down ancient and hidden artworks to bring back home. These trips together stopped with the birth of their son. Now Louise has replaced her African interests with her new Eastern passions, somehow locking JP out of her world.

"Have you ever told your wife that you miss being close to her?"

JP shakes his head vehemently, as if even considering such a conversation was far beyond any realm.

"Why not?"

"How do you imagine it? She is sitting there in her Buddha state; I do not even know if she is aware of my existence!"

"She probably isn't. Sometimes, in order to be let in, you have to knock on the door."

"You are probably right," he mumbles, and I can imagine him as a little boy in front of his father's closed door in his pyjamas, not daring to push it.

JP

It is time for JP to make real changes in his life. Since childhood he has been evolving in secretive spheres, with little or no words to name what is going on in his family. His mother was removed from his life with little or no explanation; his father retreated into his grief and shame. Then JP adopted similar attitudes with the family he built. The only way of breaking the cycle of shut doors is to start acting differently with the members of his immediate family, his wife and his son.

**

"We went to an art sale together," JP announces with pride the next time we meet.

He tells me about how excited Charles became during the auction, how he made a bid and how thrilled he was when they brought home a new piece, acquired at a reasonably good price.

"You were right after all," he volunteers reluctantly.

After the previous session hug, Charles has been passing by the gallery every day and even helped him prepare a new virtual exhibit.

"It is so strange to have him around ..."

His son's presence in the gallery has made JP realise how much that space has been terribly lonely for quite a while. His wife has been spending less and less time there, too busy with her new activities, always running with some friend to a yoga class or attending a remote meditation retreat.

"She just ignores me, I feel transparent."

"And how do you think she feels around you?"

JP is doubtful; he struggles to puzzle out what is going on in his wife's world from which he feels banned.

"I guess you want me to ask her ..."

Armed with his recent experience with Charles, he guessed right.

When we say goodbye, he looks resentful and sulky. Will he be able to follow up? Confronting his wife represents a considerable risk, and my own intuition gives a hint as to what he may be scared of finding out – maybe she is not interested anymore? After all JP has been a distant husband chasing virtual sex with the webcam girls. Maybe she has been even having an affair and will be relieved to clarify the situation and move on?

***

Next time I wait for JP to connect, he is late. A rushed WhatsApp message warns me about the delay. "I will be there in a few minutes, sorry!"

I usually avoid multiplying the communication channels with my clients, and we only use WhatsApp, which is a very personal space for many of them, when absolutely necessary. JP is using this 'emergency channel' to warn me that he is late, but maybe also about the fact that he is dealing with some out-of-the-normal situation. I am sitting in front of my screen, waiting and trying to guess again.

After ten long minutes, during which I had time to imagine a dozen possible scenarios for what is going on with him, JP's face finally lights up my screen. It takes me a few seconds to realise that it is not his face as much as his surroundings that are different – this is the very first time that I have seen him in a place other than his gallery. He is sitting in his car and the daylight pouring in from all sides is blinding. We are in the middle of the lockdown and JP is breaking the rules. This is so unlike him.

"I just could not talk to my wife," he shoots at me with the look of a naughty student.

He looks jittery and I make an attempt to calm him down. "Where are you now?"

JP looks outside, but limited by the angle of his phone's camera I can only see his face in a shaky close-up "I am in Uccle …"

"Is it where Françoise lives?"

"Yes … I just spoke to her …"

He actually went to talk to his father's partner's wife, the last person who knew his father well enough to shed some light on what was really going on behind the closed door of his office.

JP did not remember her as so tiny, but her bright blue eyes were unchanged. With her rosy dress, she looked like a moth that one finds dead in the morning by the window.

She recognised him straightaway and looked utterly unsurprised by his unannounced visit. "Here you are … I thought you would never come," she greeted him, holding the door wide open to let him into her dollhouse.

As JP sat on her flowery sofa looking at the vaguely familiar art objects neatly arranged on all available surfaces, he felt like a young boy again. Françoise told her story with ease as if both of them – her story and herself – have been waiting for him for a very long time.

"I knew you would come one day. Your late father was terribly worried about you … but you turned out well despite everything. I have always followed your gallery." As she said this, JP's eyes were scanning the room and landed on a couple of rare Lobi statuettes that he had sold for a surprisingly good price in the early days of his business. As soon as he realised that Françoise was behind that sale, which at the time was crucial for his gallery's survival, he recognised more objects, all small, but valuable that were sold to an unknown collector over the years. Each of these sales has been timely and usually would give him the courage and the means to push forward with his business.

"You have been buying from me … Why?"

"Your father and myself, we were friends, you know ... I promised him I would keep an eye on you."

"I had no idea ..."

"Your father George was a very reserved person ... but with me he talked. We often spent hours on the phone, when you were sleeping, and my husband was away. My husband frequently travelled to Africa while your father had to take care of you and your poor mother ..." As she spoke, her eyes were dreamy and tearful. JP felt strangely close to her and they ended up in an embrace, breaking all rules of social distancing. While he was holding her tiny, frail body in his arms, he suddenly felt close to his father, probably as close as never before.

JP tells me all this in one long monologue and his energy is different. Maybe I am hungry for the outside light that is filling his car's interior. It feels like a breath of a fresh air in a room that was closed for far too long ...

"When she talked about my father, it sounded like she was talking about a different person."

It was hard for JP to believe that while he was standing on the landing, cold and curious, playing out those terrible stories in his head, his father was talking with his partner's wife: "They were in love and hiding it from everybody for years!" This mystery romance was at odds with the image he had of his father, a cold and distant man who would never allow anybody into his world. For the first time, JP was able to reach beyond the façade of his secrecy and also mourn the intimacy they had never shared.

"Do you think I am doing the same with my family?"

He is finally able to make the link between his childhood experience of being locked out from his parents' world and his current self-isolation. His feeling of loneliness is a direct result of him keeping his family on the edges of his intimate world.

"The other day my wife told me that she felt left out ... I have always dreaded turning out like my father ... and now I have," he concludes bitterly.

Saying this, JP turns the key in the ignition and I can hear the sound of the engine. The car takes off and we say goodbye on the move. JP is driving back home where his wife is probably filling the void he has left with some Zen practice. The sight of her withdrawing into her inner bubble, where she insists she feels peace, reminds JP of his mother sitting on the bench of the clinic's park – with her eyes semi-closed, absent, uninterested in the outside world and in her son. There was no way for him to bring her back.

"But with Louise, I can still try?"

**

That was the last time I saw JP's face on my screen.

A few weeks later, a thick envelope arrives with my morning mail; it has a logo in the corner in the shape of an African mask. Inside I find an elegant card – an invitation to an auction of some rare masks from 'an old Belgian collection'. The lockdown has finally eased and the galleries can re-open again. On the image illustrating the sale, I recognise the masks from JP's gallery – the silent witnesses of our work.

A short hand-written note added to the invitation says: 'It is time for them to go. They have probably seen too much. Thank you!'

This is JP's way of saying goodbye to me, but also to his father.

As I read this farewell, I feel slightly hurt and, predictably, left out. I am barely surprised of being let go in the same way the webcam girls or the masks were – after all I have also seen too much of JP's inner world, and he has never grown accustomed to the discomfort this exposure brings.

In online therapy, we only interact with each other's images projected onto a screen, and the endings often feel abrupt – a door shut in the face. I do not know whether JP was able to confront his wife and if their relationship could take a new turn. Nevertheless I have to settle for this ending – respecting JP's choice, but also hoping that he has learnt to open his own doors, to let others in. Deep down I know that he has never done that with me entirely and his coming out of hiding was limited by his persistent shame that we had barely time to address.

***

A few months later, as I am enjoying my coffee on a nearby café terrace, my phone rings. I recognise the country prefix of an unknown number – 32 – Belgium. Without making the link, I follow my instinct (or curiosity) and pick up.

"Hello, it's JP again … Do you still remember me?"

Of course I do. Unfinished business has a tendency to stick around.

"I am in Paris for a few days." His still-familiar voice in its post-lockdown version sounds somehow different, more energetic.

JP wants to meet in person and I do not hide my enthusiasm as we find a slot for the next day.

Meeting for the first time after having talked for a few months from our separated lockdown spaces feels a little awkward. I open my door wide to let him in, mindful of the metaphorical value of the gesture.

"Should I keep my mask on?" We exchange a mischievous smile at the ironic subtext of his words.

"No, if you feel comfortable enough we can just keep a safe distance."

We avoid shaking hands and I open the window while JP choses one of my two identical armchairs. I take a seat while he is scrutinising my books and other objects that occupy the bookshelves – catching up on everything that was out of reach for him during our online sessions. His eyes soon stumble on an African statuette that stands at the corner of my desk.

"A nice Fang," he notices in appreciation. "I did not know you had an interest in African art."

JP is much taller than I had imagined – another consequence of the screen nature of our past interactions. Once we have caught up on the details and filled the gaps left by the camera angle, JP fills me in.

Talking with Françoise had shaken him and when he returned home from Uccle, he went straight to his wife's meditation room. She was nowhere to be found and it took him a while to realise that he had no idea about her usual whereabouts. Somehow he got all worked up in imagining that she had actually left him.

His son joined him downstairs and, in order to fight his anxiety, JP offered to cook dinner. That evening Louise returned to a surprising scene – her always-absent husband in the kitchen, washing, peeling, cutting, frying with their teenage son helping and chatting.

"That was the best evening I'd had in years," JP looks tearful as he tells me about reconnecting with his wife.

Unfortunately, it was also the last. Their new-found togetherness only lasted until they went up to their bedroom. His (and my) fantasies were not far from the truth – Louise had been having an affair with a man she had met at a yoga retreat. He was divorced, in love and eager for her to move into his vast suburban house.

"It was too late …," JP smiles sadly.

The dramatic irony was that when he was finally able to push open the door, his wife, exhausted by all the lonely waiting, had already left the room. They were on good terms though, and Louise was pleased at the way JP was turning around his relationship with Charles.

"Charles has decided to stay with me …," JP announces proudly. "We are having a lot of fun together in the gallery."

"I am pleased you came," I tell him.

Driving to Paris to enter my therapy room in person is another meaningful way for JP to practise pushing open the door in order to get what he needs.

"I have been thinking about this all along …," he admits, risking another disclosure.

"How is it for you to be here, with me in my office?"

"Less uncomfortable than I thought."

This time we say a proper goodbye, and when JP puts his mask on before stepping out into the hall, his eyes are smiling. "This is it I guess … no secret rooms anymore."

VI

Alice

London, UK

As her camera switches on, it shows a partial view over an empty corner of a room, with walls covered in white tiles – possibly a bathroom.

"Sorry, just a second." A deep, slightly familiar female voice echoes from somewhere outside the screen. Hasty steps, a faint male voice, a door closing.

"Hi." When Alice picks up the computer and stares into the camera quizzically, I recognise her face – she is a reasonably well-known actress, and I recently watched a TV series in which she played the part of a charming lawyer heavily addicted to alcohol. I make an effort to put that character aside in order to make place for the real Alice. The lockdown version of her – undone blonde hair, pale face without make-up – is strikingly different from the polished screen character that I know.

"I think I am going mad …" Alice delivers her opening line; her big transparent eyes made even bigger by the close-up image on my screen. She is fidgeting on the edge of her bathtub, her computer on her lap. The angle of the view and the dim lighting highlight her unnatural thinness. "Wait, I have to check the lock," she directs an anxious look towards the door and drops the laptop. The spotless tiled wall is all over my screen again. Alice is jumpy and paranoid, as are many who struggle with drinking.

When her face returns to my screen, she seems a little calmer. "Sorry, I had to check."

"Is this your home?"

"Yes, I live here with Alfred, my boyfriend."

"What are you scared of?"

Alice's face goes blank. "I don't really know ..."

"What about Alfred? How is your relationship?"

"It is fine. We were planning to get married this summer," she recites in a slightly robotic manner, her tense body posture contradicting her reassuring words.

"*Were* planning?"

"Are. We are planning to get married." Alice looks frozen.

"Tell me, what are you scared of?" I repeat my question, fearing the worse.

"I am scared of Alfred," she whispers and gives another quick look towards the invisible door. "Sometimes I think he could put a pillow on my face when I am asleep."

"Has he ever been physically violent with you?"

"No ..."

"What makes you fear he may be?"

"I don't know," Alice shrugs hesitantly.

They have been living together for a year now; it has been going smoothly. Until the lockdown, he travelled extensively and her working days of acting used to expand well into the night. Their limited time together was filled with social outings and exciting times with friends. But all this stopped. The show Alice was preparing for a West End theatre has been put on hold; Alfred moved a desk into their bedroom.

For a couple of weeks they enjoyed lazy mornings and long lunches, until their idyllic cocoon started showing some cracks. It began with a new script posted by her agent with a note insisting that Alice put everything aside and read it. This is exactly what she did. The lead role is tailor-made for her – a newly married woman called Rose being abused by her beloved husband.

"I just felt this was a perfect part for me. Rose is a glamorous and successful stylist – all these wonderful '50s garments, Chanel jewellery, cat's eye sunglasses … Absolutely nobody can imagine the level of abuse she is dealing with at home."

But for some reason Alfred did not feel the same way about the script. As she read him some excerpts over dinner, all excited, he frowned and seemed angry.

"He just dismissed anything I said, insisting the script was a total duff."

Alfred is an astute literary agent and Alice trusts his judgement. This is the first time they have not agreed on a project. Despite the tension between them, and maybe to show Alfred that she can judge for herself, Alice calls her agent the next day and agrees excitedly on playing Rose.

As Alice talks about her new part, she is animated and her voice changes slightly, taking on an American lilt. "Her husband is gaslighting her constantly, making her believe something is wrong with *her*!"

"Are you talking about Rose or about yourself?"

"I don't even know any more. Everything is so complicated."

As we part at the end of this initial session, I am unsure whether I should take Alice on as my client. In normal times I would probably refer her to a London-based colleague but right now in the middle of the lockdown, this is not really an option. Is she unsafe in her flat with Alfred? Or is it Alice's vivid imagination that makes her live through her character's fate?

Rattled, I google Alice's boyfriend's name – London literary agents are not that many and Alfred's name is uncommon. I stare at his honest, smiling face and feel embarrassed by what could be an unprofessional nosiness.

**

"I have signed up to the film. I am Rose now," Alice announces enthusiastically the next time we connect.

She is perched on a bench, in the middle of a park – Holland Park, she readily explains. She is wrapped up in a large shapeless knit, with flashy mid-century sunglasses on her face, defying the unfriendly greyish weather.

"We fought again and I escaped using Roxy as an alibi." She bends down disappearing from the screen and returns into the frame with a tiny Yorkshire terrier whom she kisses theatrically. "She has never had so many walks; she absolutely loves lockdown."

I ask her gently if she could take her sunglasses off and when she obeys half-heartedly, her eyes look feverish and puffy.

"Rose always had to put these on [she waves the sunglasses] to hide a black eye; everybody presumed she was just very stylish," she explains, morosely.

Alfred used to be patient with Alice when she learnt a new part, but this time is totally different. She has to hide the script, as he gets visibly annoyed every time he catches her working through its pages.

"He has changed."

"In what way?"

"He is always in a bad mood, he snaps ..."

"Have you tried to talk about it with him?"

"Yes, he says I am the one who has changed. He insists that

Rose has possessed me and is intruding into our life."

"Has she possessed you?"

"A bit ...," she smiles mischievously, "but this always happens when I take on a new part."

I can see Alfred's point. Alice does seem to be taken over by her character. But then, is it that unusual for an actress? I did not know her before this role, so I cannot really tell whether her personality has changed.

"Did Alfred complain in the past about your way of becoming one with the characters you play?"

"No, he never did. We used to joke about my drinking when I played that alcoholic lawyer ... Why does he dislike Rose so much? She has done nothing wrong, apart from choosing the wrong guy."

"Have you asked him?"

"I tried, but he wouldn't talk ... Why do you ask?" she stares into the camera suspiciously.

Alfred's attitude towards Alice's new role sounds odd, but the stress with the current exceptional circumstances could explain it. I decide to shift the focus on Alice herself; I am still unclear about what is really going on with her.

"Do you know why you were chosen to play Rose?"

"The director liked me in my last role ... It was also a woman dealing with a lot of crap," Alice offers somewhat defensively.

"And what about your own past? Is there anything from what is happening to Rose that resonates with you?"

"If there is, the director would not know about it."

"But you do know about it, right?"

Alice looks away, then puts Rose's sunglasses back on.

The sun is going down and our time is almost up. I am painfully aware of her being alone and exposed in the middle of a public park. This is not an ideal situation to address anything painful or traumatic – but now I am certain that there is something significant in her past that Alice has not told me about. Not yet.

Before we end, I ask Alice to make sure she connects from a more private place.

"Do you miss my bathroom?" she replies mockingly in an attempt to lighten up the tone. I hope she finds a way despite the lockdown.

***

As I wait for her in front of my computer, I am thinking about Rose and all those women who, right now, are trapped in a closed space with their abuser, with nowhere else to go.

When Alice finally connects, her video is off, and I start to fear that she is hiding some bad bruises.

"Sorry, I am in a taxi, on my way to the airport," she clarifies in a rushed voice, and I exhale in relief. "My mother's neighbour called this morning to say she has tested positive with Covid, but doesn't want me to know."

After making the neighbour swear that she would keep her arrival secret, Alice booked the first flight to Guernsey, a British island tucked in the middle of the Channel between England and France. She has not been back to 'the Rock' in years, and I am unsure how much of her anxiety is due to her mother's condition or to her forced return to her birthplace.

"At least, this gave me a way out of that flat!" she sighs, but there is no relief in her voice.

"I guess we cannot have a proper session during your drive to the airport; shall we meet when you are settled there?"

Alice keeps silent for a moment and I can distinguish the noise of a motorway and a distant radio playing a pop tune.

"I will let you know." The uncertain notes in her voice leave me with many questions about her past, her mother and her commitment to figuring this out in therapy or not.

***

Next time we connect, I am introduced to another bathroom. From what I can see, this one is grim and out-of-date, even a bit dirty. The small window in the granite wall lets in an uncertain morning light. In her oversized pyjama top, Alice seems thinner than usual.

"How is your mother?"

"Not that bad, she's a tough cookie." Her smile contradicts the look of her transparent feverish eyes.

"And what about you?"

"I hate being stuck in this rabbit hole," she concedes. "This horrid house stinks," she adds, scrutinising the bathroom with disgust.

"What does it smell of?"

"Fried fish. Alcohol …" she stares out of the window.

"Alcohol?"

"My mother likes her gin," she adds with defiance. Alice's addicted lawyer role comes back to me.

"How long has she been drinking?"

"I am not sure … I was young … as far as I can remember, she always had a glass of gin or Prosecco within reach, whatever she was doing."

Alice has little recollection of those early years. Often sick and bed-ridden, she used to spend long days off school, watching from her bedroom the seagulls wailing and fighting for food above a restaurant's kitchen. The restaurant's brick wall was hiding the sea, only visible from her mother's upstairs bedroom.

Even now, as we talk, seagulls' squawks reach us from outside, difficult to ignore, similar to those of a crying child.

"This place never changes, it is as freaking cold as I remember it," Alice shivers.

"When was the last time you visited the island?"

"Years ago ... and I haven't missed it."

Alice has no friends remaining on the island; they have all left and made a life elsewhere. 'The Rock' was too small for young women ready to take the plunge into adult life; but to get out of there, one had to cross the Channel. It was an easy crossing for wealthier families, who would send their children off to posh boarding schools in the UK; for Alice this was out of reach. Her mother worked at the local supermarket and made just enough money to pay the mortgage and see them both to the end of the month.

"Alice!" A coarse female voice calls from the bowels of the cottage, making Alice frown annoyingly.

"Wait a sec. I'm coming," she screams surprisingly loudly towards the door, and for a second I regret having earphones plugged deep in my ears.

"Is she still drinking?"

"She is ... When I came, she was barricaded inside and would not let me in. She pretended she did not want me to catch the virus, but I could tell she was plastered and wanted me out of the way," she says angrily, and then looks away.

"Alice, growing up with an addicted parent is harsh ... Did you have any other family around?"

"No. My mother came here to work as a nurse just before I was born; her family stayed back in Ireland."

She lets her long hair fall over her face, hiding her tears from view. "She did not wait for Covid to self-isolate in her room. This is exactly what she has done all the time ... with a bottle of wine."

"And you could not compete with that bottle, right?"

She shrugs and looks crushed. I have no time to respond as

a doorbell makes us both jump.

"The wine delivery, I am sure. How could she run out of booze?" she explains bitterly and opens the small window to peek outside. The seagulls' anxious screaming gets louder – the soundtrack of Alice's lonely childhood days. "I have to go, sorry!"

I have no choice but to leave her there, dealing with the wine delivery and her reckless mother.

***

When I see Alice again she wears a black turtleneck sweater, her hair is collected elegantly in a high bun and her face is made up subtly.

"Sorry for the mess." She looks around in disarray. "There is only one bathroom in this house and my mother hates my attempts to tidy up."

The bathroom looks even scruffier in the daylight. Alice's neat appearance creates a dissonance with the setting.

"How is your mother?"

"Coughing, but well enough to have her drink."

Something about the bathroom rattles me. Why does Alice choose to connect from this confined space again? She is visibly embarrassed about it and for a reason – I can almost smell the unwashed clothes that are piled up behind her back.

"And what about your childhood room?"

"What about it? It is still there, cluttered with stuff."

"Why do you prefer to connect from here?" I ask, hoping for a useful clue.

She shrugs in dismissal. "I don't know … the connection is better," she offers, almost lightly.

Is it? It is actually pretty unstable and soon her camera freezes, forcing us to re-start the call.

"I am working on my part again." She takes advantage of one such technical interruption to steer away from my initial question. "This island is an ideal place to self-isolate after all." I resist commenting, despite my already rampant curiosity.

"Alfred keeps calling … He wants to join me here." She offers me another distraction from the topic of her childhood room.

"How do you feel about him coming?"

"I prefer to keep him away from this place."

"Does he know about your mother's drinking?"

"Only vaguely …"

As I look at her shaky face, which takes over my screen, I notice the dark shadows under her eyes that the make-up can barely hide.

"How is your sleep?"

"Horrible," she admits. "I keep having these stupid nightmares …" she explains, angrily. "I hate this creepy place."

"Could you tell me about the nightmares?"

She stays silent for a moment and I can sense her fear, which somehow creeps into my room, into my body.

"I thought they had stopped …"

"Have they just resumed since your return here?"

"The worse thing about them is that I am half-awake but paralysed, unable to move," she acquiesces reluctantly.

We sit in silence together for a few long moments, as Alice plucks up her courage. I hope that having me around when she returns to that scary place can help Alice to face what she has been trying to process through these repeated nightmares for years.

"It always starts with the steps … Heavy steps in the corridor … I am lying in bed in a cold sweat, terrorised and unable to move. The steps stop at the door of my bedroom. I lie still, as still as possible, praying for them to continue beyond my door. Sometimes they do. But sometimes they don't and then the door opens slowly

..." Alice, unable to continue, stops. Her hands join her hair in the effort to hide her face. I can tell that she is not breathing; her hands are shaking.

"Alice, let's take a deep breath. You are here with me and now you are safe," I say to her as my heart is racing, following hers.

She inhales deeply a few times and calms down a little. "It is just a stupid dream, right?"

"Do you know whose steps they are?" I ask and she shakes her head vehemently "No, I never see the person who opens the door … and I am terrified I may discover his face."

"Is there a part of you who wishes you could see him though?"

She nods almost invisibly, looking exhausted.

"And if we imagine that you can make it to under your bed and watch this person opening the door from the safety of your hiding spot?"

"I never thought about this," she responds, surprised by my suggestion.

"Maybe you could try next time … If the nightmare comes back, of course?"

She agrees promptly and we are both sure that the steps will return to haunt her.

Our time is almost up. I decide to leave it there for now, almost relieved to pause our quest until Alice's next weekly session.

***

"I couldn't stand being locked in that house any more …" Alice is perched on a granite rock; behind her head the sky is surprisingly bright. The strong wind is blowing her hair from all sides, in a vain effort to undo her blonde ponytail. Seagulls' alarmed squawking and the blowing wind fill all the space between us.

"They've forecast a storm coming from the mainland …"

UNLOCKED

Her watercolour eyes seem to have borrowed the greyness of the surrounding elements. They scrutinise a horizon that I can only guess at. "They have called it Rose," she smiles.

We both feel relieved to be in the open. I make a mental note about Alice distracting me again with another even more dramatic setting. Is this just another way she is avoiding her childhood bedroom?

"Are you sure you are safe out there?"

"Certainly safer than anywhere else ... I have always come here to escape from everything." Her gaze goes towards the unseen waves I can hear beating against the rocks. "There is something I haven't told you ..." she looks away, and her words are fading in the raging wind. She goes silent for a long minute and the shaky phone in her hands adds to my fear of seeing her blown away from this rock, falling into the turbulent Channel waters.

"There was a kind of father I had one time ... my mother's boyfriend Tim ... I was very attached to him. But one day he disappeared. I remember being heartbroken."

'He left the island' was her mother's dry explanation and, for a long time after him vanishing, Alice kept dreaming about joining him in faraway lands. For several years after that, each time she saw the ferry heading towards the mainland, she would picture them both standing on the deck, holding hands. She imagined him settling in Australia or New Zealand, having other kids, playing with them as he used to play with her.

"At times I've imagined he drowned during the crossing ..."

Her mother would never mention the vanished boyfriend. Soon enough, Alice learnt to avoid saying his name, to keep her mother from 'overdoing it again' and pouring her alcohol-loaded anger at her. She could not find a picture of Tim in their house,

112

even as she searched methodically her mother's bedroom one day. All the hiding places that she knew of were empty, except for a few unfinished bottles of gin.

Her mother seemed consistently angry with men who came into her life after him – her co-workers from the supermarket, her neighbours, her girlfriends' husbands …

"How old were you when Tim left the island?"

"Seven or eight … I remember feeling very lonely once he was gone." This is exactly how young Alice looks right now on my screen, her wet hair sticking to her reddened cheeks – a third grader skipping school.

Around that time, her mother's drinking got worse and Alice had to take care of herself. "This is when this particular rock became my best hiding place; I would sit here for hours, looking at the ferryboats leaving the harbour, picturing myself on board, looking back at the shrinking island for the last time …"

"Have you ever asked your mother about what happened to Tim?"

Alice shakes her head. "No, I have always kept away from it … Do you think I should?"

I am unsure what to respond. Tim's sudden and unexplained disappearance created such a void for Alice to fill with cravings that her drunk mother was not able to satisfy – warmth, safety and intimacy – that she probably idealised this vanishing figure from her early childhood.

"As you grew up, why didn't you press your mother for more information about Tim?"

Alice considers my question, watching the stormy sea. "Maybe I was scared that she would tell me something I did not want to hear …"

The sound of pouring rain suddenly erupts into my room and

on the other end of the line I watch the sky coming down in a heavy shower, making Alice jump up and run towards shelter. We disconnect in a rush, before saying our goodbyes or planning for the next session. My screen goes blank, but the sound of crashing waves and howling winds stays with me for some time.

**

A few days later, an email from Alice reads: "My mother's drinking is out of control. I think she needs help. Could we discuss urgently please?"

It is early morning and I am checking my phone while absorbing my bucket of strong coffee in my office. With every new lockdown, waking up has become more challenging. A bleak mid-winter light is coming in from the eerily silent outside. As I read her twitchy words, a daunting sense of responsibility comes upon me. The coffee tastes bitter, and Saint-Exupéry's words pop into my head: 'Tu es responsable de ce que tu as apprivoisé – You become responsible, forever, for what you have tamed'. I type in a quick answer to Alice, offering to meet over my lunch break.

I do not regret skipping lunch as I am finally allowed into her childhood bedroom. Alice is cramped on a single bed, a fluffy blanket on her shoulders. "It is really cold in here," she mutters, holding her laptop close to her chest, her face even closer up than usually. Her girly bed is tightly tucked against the wall covered with dusty flowery wallpaper.

"Yesterday my mother seemed better. She was almost sober and she cooked fried fish for dinner," Alice starts her narrative, sounding younger and even more vulnerable than usual. "This was the first time in years that we had shared a meal she'd cooked … At the end I asked her about Tim."

"He was not what he seemed," her mother cut her short. Then she left the table, taking the unfinished bottle of wine with her. Since then she has barely left her bedroom and, based on the empty bottles piling up in the kitchen, Alice can tell that she has been drinking heavily.

"She has not been this bad in years. Do you think it is all because I mentioned Tim?"

"It's possible," I nod, as I hardly believe heavy drinking occurs without a reason. We stay silent for a few moments, considering our options.

"Has your mother ever sought help for her addiction?" I ask, guessing the answer already. The smaller the community, the harder it is for someone caught up in drinking to reach out for treatment.

"Are you joking? She couldn't bear the idea of people finding out about what is going on in here," she confirms my intuition. "As if nobody ever guessed …," she adds angrily.

In front of Alice's mother's drinking, we both feel deflated.

"What about your role? How is it going?" I bring her back to her present life, where she enjoys an agency and freedom that were not attainable during her secluded childhood.

"I have been struggling with Rose," she admits sadly. "Talking with Alfred does not help," she adds with a surprisingly mischievous sparkle in her eyes.

He is now calling every night and they have long conversations, as they have not had in months. For some reason, with the Channel between them, Alfred has returned to the pre-lockdown version of himself.

"He is now surprisingly supportive about my project; he asks about Rose, and seems genuinely interested … It is so disorientating."

"Any thoughts about this transformation?"

"He returned to see his therapist," she admits with an ironic smile, and I return her smile, as some weight slips off my shoulders.

"You know, he told me about his family ... things that he had never shared before ... I had no clue," she admits in bewilderment.

Alfred's mother had to flee from his father, who was physically violent with her and their small son. She then remarried a decent man who became a caring stepfather for Alfred. But the early memories of his mother crying and the escape from their home, hiding at neighbours or friends, have stuck with him forever.

"When I brought Rose home, all this old trauma was awakened, or at least this is what his therapist said," Alice tells me with an infectious relief.

I have not had time to comment when a loud banging interrupts us, making me jump. Alice looks surprisingly unperturbed. "It's my mother. This is how she lets me know that she needs more alcohol. She is banging on the pipe that runs between our rooms. That is how she has always done it."

My jaw drops, as the banging grows more insistent.

"I should probably go and get her more wine before she breaks something or hurts herself," Alice sighs and puts the blanket away. "I couldn't imagine letting anybody see this ... I am sorry."

I feel for her as her usually pale face flashes with shame at the display of her family despair. "Did she do that when you were young?"

She nods, letting her hair fall over her face. I wish I could go back in time and rescue her from this misery.

"This time you are not alone there."

"I know. I have Alfred ... and you ... Do you think I could ask my mother to join us next time?"

I am taken aback by her question. I cannot say I would welcome her mother in our protective space. "It is a long shot ... but we can try," I finally agree. This could be a unique opportunity for Alice to confront her mother in front of a witness.

"What would you like to get out of it?"

"To make her speak ... about Tim."

We have to seal the deal quickly as the banging is getting more impatient, making any further discussion impossible.

**

This time Alice connects from a bigger, brighter room – the family sitting room, I guess. By now, I must have visited every room in the cottage, except for her mother's upstairs bedroom.

"My mother agreed to join us. She should be with us in a few moments," she announces, fidgeting in her chair.

"Wonderful. I am glad we can talk all together," I respond, trying my best to contain my own anxiety. I was not expecting her mother to go along with this, and certainly not before we could have prepared for this together with Alice.

"I hope she hasn't drunk ... or at least, not too much," she adds, echoing my own worry, as she brings in a second chair in front of the computer.

"We have just received the results of her last Covid test, finally negative," she shares with relief. "And I have already booked my flight back."

I have no time to react. In the background a door opens and an even thinner, blonder version of Alice makes it into the room. She wears light-blue joggers, a matching hoodie and a facemask.

Alice offers her mother a seat and introduces her; I learn that the woman's name is Pam. This is certainly the first time I see a patient wearing a mask during a video session.

"So, you are the Parisian shrink who is digging into my past?"

she snaps, angrily, skipping all niceties.

I have no idea what is happening under her mask, but Pam's lustreless eyes scream inner turmoil.

As soon as her coarse voice and her emotional struggle fill the space between us, I am free of my anxiety about meeting her.

"I guess I am. Pleased to meet you," I start lightly.

"My daughter has dragged me here, I have no idea why," she announces grumpily, making Alice cringe and me smile inside. Pam is resolved to stay shut; she makes me think of a clam washed out by the ocean.

"I do know why, and I believe you do too, but we can ask her again," I come back at her with firmness. Trying to meet Alice's eyes (not easy through our respective cameras), I invite her to step in. She mumbles something, uneasy with her mother's edgy presence.

"I think Alice wants to find out what happened to your former boyfriend Tim, to whom she was very attached as a child. I believe he disappeared without warning or explanation ... "

"This is an old story and none of your business," she snaps, and now I can tell that she has had more than one drink. Not ideal for a confrontation, but this is a unique opportunity and I have to use it.

"Alice, do you want to say something to your mother?" I make another attempt at bringing Alice in.

"Yes. I do ... Mum, Tim was the only man who was kind and caring with me. When he left without any notice, I felt completely abandoned."

"He was not what he seemed, I told you," she repeats stubbornly, and even the mask cannot conceal the contortion of her features.

"Mum, but what does that mean? Why were you so selfish? Have you ever thought about me?"

"I did. I did think about you and that is exactly why the only decent man I ever met had to go!" Pam finally pulls off her mask, showing her reddened face, very like Alice's, although hardened by years of heavy drinking and solitude.

"Now, if you *really* want to know, I will tell you what happened." Once she's started, Pam cannot stop. "One day I felt sick and came back from work early. Tim was nowhere to be found. You were off school, with one of those awful anginas. I came to check on you and what did I find? Tim in your bed, his pants on the floor ..." Once her secret spills out, Pam deflates; all her anger and defensiveness are gone. Liberated tears run down her unmasked face.

Alice looks at her mother in silence, her expressive face displaying a whole array of emotions at once – disbelief, horror, anger, hurt and finally pity.

"Mum ... Did you tell anybody?"

"No, I did not. You know how the Rock is ... My life here would have been destroyed. Everybody would have known about it ... I had to protect you. I gave him one day to pack and get off the island."

"I don't remember anything ..." Alice stares at me in dismay.

"You were only eight ... Eight!" Pam screams.

"It is not unusual to suppress traumatic memories, and you were very young," I try to reassure her.

"I missed him so much," Alice looks utterly confused.

"I missed him too, that bastard." There is no confusion in Pam's voice, only anger and regret.

The golden light of sunset and the seagulls' calls make it to my office again. Shame emanating from Alice's mother, even filtered by the distance and technology, ties them up with its heavy dark shroud. Alice stares at the screen, but I do not think she is looking at me – her eyes are shiny and absent. Pam looks away, avoiding being seen by either her daughter or myself. I sit back and let them process the heavy secret that has just been unleashed.

"Why haven't you told me?" Alice finally breaks the shame-filled silence.

"I hoped you wouldn't remember." Pam's tears are now running freely down her cheeks.

"I did not …"

"If only you knew how many times I lay in bed, trying to un-see what I had seen … I wanted so badly to forget!" she shrugs in disgust. "And I wanted to spare you this," she groans.

Alice covers her face with her hands in an attempt to disappear.

"Is this what you wanted?" Pam gawks at me with such an intense hatred that I automatically recoil in my chair.

"No, I did not want this, and I do not enjoy witnessing pain," I say, and I mean it. "But we cannot pretend it didn't happen."

"Why? Alice didn't remember. The guy was gone," Pam stubbornly refuses to concede.

"He betrayed your trust, your child's trust, and this has had a huge impact on your life and on your relationship with your only daughter."

"What are you talking about?" Pam looks away but I can tell she is ready to hear more.

"I am talking about your drinking."

"What does it have to do with this? And it's none of your business."

"You have already told me that, but I do not agree. I care for Alice and she happens to be your daughter. Your drinking has been affecting her, taking her only parent away."

"Mum, I hated you for your drinking, I could not understand why …" Alice finally steps in.

"Now you know why," Pam concedes, all her aggressiveness gone.

"Mum, I needed you and you were always drunk, locked in your room."

"When he was gone, I couldn't tell anybody. You kept crying and asking about him, my friends kept nagging me about the wedding that I had been stupid enough to announce … I just didn't know what to tell them, and the worse thing was that I missed him too."

"Pam, I am sorry about what happened to your daughter and to you, but it is probably time to limit the damage."

"How so? Will you make me travel back in time to avoid meeting him altogether?" Behind her sarcasm I am sensing a faint hope.

"No, therapy can't do this for you, but it can help you curb your drinking, and have a chance to build a better relationship with your daughter; Alice still needs a mother."

"She does not; tomorrow she will be back to London and will forget about me and the island again."

"Mum, she is right." Alice is now ready to meet her mother's eyes, but Pam keeps staring at the screen.

Alice and her mother sit motionless, like two statues made from the same person, their shoulders touching, in order to fit into my screen.

***

Seeing Alice in her childhood bedroom again takes me aback. This time she is sitting on the floor, her back against the flowery wall.

"You are still in Guernsey?" I show my surprise.

"I am … stuck on the Rock again," she responds with a sad irony. "I could not leave my mother alone, not in this state. Since our conversation she has been really shaken."

"How are *you* doing with what you have discovered?"

"I am ok, I guess ... I still don't remember anything really, apart from missing Tim and feeling lonely," she shrugs. "And yet I have no doubt that my mother is telling the truth. She was really in love with that guy ... I was lying in bed last night, trying to remember ... but nothing came up, I just felt trapped and confused." She scrutinises her bedroom walls as if hoping they would recall the events from over twenty years ago.

"This is most probably how you felt as a child, when Tim came to your bed," I suggest.

"This is the exact same bed I had when I was eight. After our last session, I couldn't get into it any more ... I ended up sleeping on the floor," she stares at the childhood bed that I cannot see. "I probably should get rid of it before I leave." Excellent idea, I think, as Alice continues with more energy. "I remember asking for a double bed, but my mother wouldn't buy me one. I don't understand why ... This one would have reminded her of Tim, why not get rid of it?"

My guess is that the idea of a double bed for her daughter was unbearable to Pam, too close to the image imprinted on her mind of her own man assaulting her child.

For Pam, this bed still standing in her empty daughter's room has been a tangible reminder of her boyfriend's betrayal, a constant activator of shame that has been consuming her ever since. No amount of alcohol can make it go away; every drink she absorbs feeds this shame like a powerful fertiliser.

"You could probably ask her why." I know they will have to have other conversations about the whole topic, painful but hopefully healing for both of them.

"Do you think I should try harder to remember what happened with Tim?"

"Do you want to remember?"

We sit in silence for a few long moments as Alice is grappling with this recently acquired childhood trauma.

"No, I don't," she acknowledges. "Should I?"

"No, you don't have to."

Alice exhales with relief.

"We cannot go back in time and change what happened. What we can do is make sure childhood abuse does not get in the way of your achieving things that you want in your present life."

"I don't think this has ever stopped me from doing anything," she shakes her head with energy.

"Are you sure?"

"I am not sure of anything anymore ..." She picks up her blanket from the floor and pulls it onto her shoulders. "I had that nightmare again ..." she shivers. I can see that she is desperate again to escape from that room.

"Can you guide me into your dream?" I offer, mindful that this is probably the last time we will have access to her childhood bedroom.

"This time, when the steps stopped behind the door, I hid under the bed ..."

"Let's close our eyes, and I will join you there, hiding under the bed." I close my eyes first. Darkness fills everything, and Alice's voice sounds younger and increasingly anxious as she continues.

"I can almost hear his breathing, it is heavy and it smells ... of the fried fish that we have had for lunch ... His hand turns the door handle." The panic in her voice invades my own body. We lie under the bed, surrounded by darkness and dust. I would like to hold her hand, as I sense her shaking.

"He opens the door and lets himself in ... I close my eyes very tightly. I hope he will not see me, 'Where is my little prawn?' he says as he enters the room. But the bed is empty. And this is where I decide to wake up, and I do wake up."

"Of course, it is empty; we are both lying under the bed." I open my eyes in relief. We stare at each other for a few seconds.

"That was spooky," she says.

"It was," I agree.

"It is so weird. I saw Tim's face clearly. I remember him now."

"I could feel how scared and trapped you felt in that room." I am still grappling with what we have just experienced.

She nods sadly.

"That was terribly wrong." I cannot find other words as anger starts filling my guts. "You were just a child and you trusted him completely."

"What a bastard," she admits angrily as her breathing gets heavier.

"Maybe it is time to get rid of this bed?" I want to use the energy of her newly discovered rage.

"You are right. Wait a second." She leaves the laptop on the floor, stands up, letting the blanket slip from her shoulders, and disappears from my screen. Her camera now shows a corner of her room, the pink peony of the wallpaper and the chink of an open window.

I can hear some movement, then the sound of something breaking, and a heavy object being dragged along the floor. Then Alice reappears in the frame with what looks like wooden bits of the bed and throws them one after another out of the window.

When her face makes it back to the screen, her cheeks are red and her eyes are shining.

"Job done," she concludes with satisfaction. I do not hide my enthusiasm as we both hear Pam's voice grumbling downstairs over the broken furniture.

***

"So, you are back home," I state the obvious when Alice connects from what looks like the immaculate living room of her London flat.

"I am," she admits with a smile, showing me Roxy, comfortably nestled on her lap. "So relieved to be back," she sighs.

"How is your mother?"

"You will not believe it, but we ended up burning the bed together in the garden that night," she confesses and I can sense that behind her amusement there is a deep relief.

"I am sorry I missed that," I say honestly.

"Thank you for talking with my mother. We had never spoken like that together. I promised to ask you if you could suggest a therapist for her," she smiles. "Who could have thought I would ever say these words ..."

"Well, I happen to know somebody in Guernsey whom I can highly recommend to your mother."

Once that was out the way, I ask my burning question: "What about Alfred? How do you feel about being back with him?"

Alice thinks carefully before responding, "It is very strange, but things seem just back to normal. How is that possible?"

She looks at me waiting for an explanation, and this time I have one to offer. "If I understood it correctly, you started feeling trapped at the beginning of the lockdown, right?"

"We are still pretty much locked down, but I am no longer scared of him."

Alice stares at the screen in confusion as I keep going; the risk of getting it wrong is probably smaller than the potential benefit if I get it right.

"You had also mentioned that your wedding day was getting

closer?" It is her turn to nod silently. "Just like your mother and Tim," I draw the now obvious parallel. "When we started meeting you were confused and suspicious of Alfred, right?" She nods again. "Now when you think about the betrayal that you experienced with Tim – the only man that you had trusted and loved in your childhood – your fear of letting Alfred too close, literally into your bed and deeper into your life, makes sense."

Alice listens with intense interest, her eyes riveted to the screen. "So, it wasn't just Rose … It is true that, even with my earlier relationships, I always freaked out and broke up just before it could get serious," she admits. "Does it mean I can never trust a man? I really want it to work out with Alfred."

"Now that you know where this distrust may have come from, it is up to you to decide whether you want to give this relationship a chance."

"I do want to give Alfred a chance and I don't want Tim to take this away from me," she concludes.

This is the note we end on this time. Alice switches off, leaving me alone, my room slowly sinking into the bluish dusk of the Parisian evening. The blurred face of a man that I've worked hard to forget forces itself back into my mind. Something in my body becomes instantly tight and cold. Even after years of therapy, this flashback catches me off guard.

The warm laughter of my husband and my daughter reach me from the other side of our flat, and I suddenly feel a sharp relief about not having let him take that away from me.

***

I meet with Alice for a few more times. Her film project is now in a more intense phase and she is fully taken up by Rose. I observe how she brings to the sessions Rose's mannerisms, her bright stylish outfits, but also her fear and her hurt. But now the line separating Alice from Rose is clear and we can laugh about her character popping into the therapy room with us.

"She could clearly do with some therapy," Alice says. Her experience of childhood abuse is now informing her acting, giving her version of Rose a deeply personal edge.

***

A few weeks after our final session, Pam emails me about her personal therapy: she 'would rather talk to somebody online, maybe from the mainland'. She could eventually meet them in person when she travels to London to see her daughter. "That would be so much easier," she adds. "I just don't trust local shrinks." The disdain in her tone can barely cover up the shame she feels about not having been able to better protect her daughter and her years of drinking.

***

Several months later, I come across an article about the upcoming release of the film starring Alice.

"Rose gave me courage to confront my own story," she declares in the interview. "Playing this part was challenging in many ways, but also deeply rewarding."

Reading her words I smile; being with Alice through the worse months of the pandemic put me in a privileged position. I am probably the only person who knows *how* challenging playing Rose has been for her. In reinventing her character's story, she had to face her own past and rewrite her own narrative. I am very proud of Alice and cannot wait to see the film – a rare artefact, a kind of journal of our therapeutic journey.

VII

Claudio

Rome, Italy

This time the wind is blowing, its furious gusts bursting into my earphones in loud waves. Claudio – early forties, boyish round face, dark curls escaping from a black baseball cap – is sitting on the grass, his back against a kind of tree that I know – a scrap of familiarity in the middle of this unsettled setting.

"I had to get the hell out of there!" he explains.

The bright Italian sun reminds me of better days and I can barely resist saying thank you for taking me out.

Claudio has been connecting from this park, mainly consisting of umbrella pine trees, since the beginning of the lockdown. At first, this choice struck me as surprising, since he has no partner to deal with, no pet to walk. At first sight he enjoys the regular and comfortable life of a reasonably successful professional.

"I hate joggers," he comments, looking sideways at several men and women in bright outfits, who I spot running on the sidewalk.

I have never seen the full camera image of Claudio's body, and he has not mentioned his weight, but I figure him out to be overweight. When I ask him about his exercise routine, he brushes it away: "I hate the gym, don't ever try to force me there." There is something awkward about the way he moves his body that makes me wonder whether he has ever exposed it naked to someone.

As he stares at the joggers with disdain, I decide to push it a little further. "Have you ever wished to be one of them, strolling among other fit people?"

"Why would I?" he looks at me with disbelief and I step back, wary of shaming him for not being one of those slim people. We hit a dead end, again.

With Claudio, the dead and loose ends abound. I regularly stumble on his silences, his sarcasm or his stubborn refusal to talk about any potentially challenging topic. After our sessions I often feel exhausted as if I have just run a race that he is refusing to even consider.

"I used to play football," he announces out of the blue.

"When was that?" I am not particularly interested in team games but Claudio rarely volunteers information and my curiosity is piqued.

"At school … but that was a long time ago," he responds and peers back into the camera. "But what I actually wanted to talk about is this girl I met on the app a few days ago …" He jumps back to his favourite topic.

Claudio has never been in a romantic relationship, apart from some fantasy ones. In our first conversation he mentioned one teenage crush (she was too popular to notice him) and a series of romantic infatuations, short-lived and mostly illusory.

"Her name is Eva. She lives in Odessa," he announces defiantly.

"Is it even her real name?" I wonder silently.

Based on his previous experience with the same dating website, I easily guess the rest: she is too young, too beautiful and their exchanges are limited to some vaguely sexual images and arrays of emoticons, because she does not speak Italian or English.

Claudio has for years been an habitué of one of those websites specialising in Eastern European brides. He has never gone as far as meeting one of these women, but has had a few virtual crushes that somehow mask the total absence of romantic relationships in his life. Since the beginning of the lockdown, his obsession with this illusory dating has grown. He has studied pictures of the potential brides for hours and spent large sums of money on sending flowers or other services offered by the website.

"Claudio, do you think that Eva is likely to be interested in a relationship with you?"

"Why do you have to be so pessimistic?"

Every time I attempt to challenge his obsession with unattainable women, Claudio gets defensive and fights back. "I thought you would be more understanding than Italian therapists ...," he tells me reproachfully. In my foreignness he finds some comfort. Even if we use his mother tongue to communicate, my accent allows him to feel less threatened: I am not an Italian woman and should be less judgemental on his preference for East European women.

"Let me show you her picture," he looks through his phone; his face disappears, replaced by a black window.

"Please, do not," I try to interrupt but Claudio is stubbornly following his own agenda. Had we been sitting in my therapy room, I could have pointed out the 'no mobile phone' policy, but he is out there, in a Roman park, all by himself, resolved to fully use the power that this set-up provides him.

A few seconds later, a sound announces an image landing into my chat box. I obediently click on the message – another forced smile and a pair of childish blue eyes appear on my screen; the heavy make-up and a well-studied pose point towards a staged picture, probably shot in the same studio as all the other girls he has forced me to look at before. All of them share that woman-child look of some Italian Renaissance Madonna, which creates a mesmerising effect on young and innocent males.

"Claudio, why do you think you keep chasing these surreal creatures that live on the other side of Europe, and whose language you do not speak, when in Rome there are probably thousands of nice, smart, single women, interested in a relationship with someone like you?"

This is not the first time I have put this question to him. He always finds a way of brushing it away. "The local market is competitive, all the beauties are already taken by the rich and famous," he jokes in his most annoying, self-deprecating manner. "And what is left for a guy like me?" His hands illustrate this rhetorical question by a movement, which reminds me of a big bird scared off by a hunter.

"A guy like you?"

"You know what I mean," he mumbles, threatened by the seriousness of my tone.

"No, I do not. I have the impression that the person I see is somehow different from the person you feel you are." I know he will not take the risk to ask exactly how I perceive him, so I decide to take this further: "I see a sensitive young man who has been lonely for a long time."

For a second his face loses all barriers, the usual smirk is replaced by a timid smile. But the vulnerability is cleared away in a second, replaced by the regular mixture of irony and disdain.

"Then Eva should appreciate what I have to offer," he concludes with a provocative grin.

Unfortunately we both know that Eva, limited by distance and the linguistic barrier, probably perceives exactly what Claudio is internally struggling with: his image altered by shame, a miserable, overweight and ageing loner.

"So, would you like to tell me, who do you see in the mirror?"

"A weirdo," he drops and stares at me angrily. "Happy?"

"I am not happy," I acknowledge, "but if this is how you feel, I understand a bit better the reason why you do not take the risk of getting closer to any real and potentially available woman."

He looks away in embarrassment.

"Claudio, I would like to understand why you ended up feeling this way." I offer us a goal, and he nods, without looking at the screen.

"We have a plan then," I state and hope that we will be able to stick to it.

***

Next time I switch on the camera, secretly looking forward to my weekly portion of Roman Spring, Claudio connects from indoors. His heavy body is awkwardly stuck between an empty wall and the desk. Without his usual baseball cap, his balding is obvious.

"It's raining today," he grumpily explains the change of scenery.

I can tell that he is edgy, unsettled.

"Is it uncomfortable for you to let me into your flat via the video?"

He stares above the top of the screen and his face expresses disgust, the same emotion he usually conceals when he jokes about himself.

"Women do not show up here too often …," he recognises. "But don't expect too much of it!", he snaps in a surprisingly aggressive manner.

I am taken aback, slightly embarrassed about my own curiosity about his interior. Meeting with clients through the webcam has taught me to pay attention to their surroundings and open my senses to what they decide to show, consciously or not, to make me understand their story.

"I should probably clean up," he acknowledges, "but right now, with the lockdown, what's the use? Nobody comes here anyway."

"And before the lockdown, how often did you have guests?"

"My mother comes around sometimes … She is obsessed with cleaning the place."

With the travelling restrictions, Eva cannot come to Rome and Claudio does not seem to regret it – he is probably not ready to invite her to his town, his flat or his life anyway. He has been resourceful in building barriers around himself. Flirting with women thousands of miles away has kept him from any risk of invasion, and his cluttered interior protects him from too much scrutiny, and too much shame.

"My mother is a saint, really …" Invasive, but easy to keep at bay, she is an annoying but necessary part of Claudio's existence.

She constantly reminds her only son that she is desperate for grandchildren; in the same conversation she usually complains about modern women knowing nothing about housekeeping: "not even able to make a decent plate of pasta." Claudio eats dinner with her every Friday, when he drops his weekly laundry off for her old housekeeper to take care of.

"I haven't been to her place for weeks," Claudio sighs with relief. "She is too scared of catching the virus." The pandemic gives him a break from his filial duties. He orders her groceries online; she calls him daily to enquire about his diet.

Claudio's dead father seems to sit on top of the family Olympus mountain. Claudio followed him into the same career, architecture, and, when he died several years ago, Claudio inherited his decent-size architecture *studio*, which he is now trying to keep afloat, despite 'difficult times'.

Claudio has never left the old neighbourhood of Trastevere, in which he grew up. His parents' *attico*, designed by his father as a showcase, is just around the corner from his current flat. Since his teenage years he has also been dreaming about leaving Italy, escaping to a place where he could start all over again: Thailand or Belorussia ... somewhere where the women are young, beautiful and undemanding.

***

At the beginning of the following session, Claudio mentions a job posting at a large architecture firm, looking for a director for a big project in Dubai. "It is tempting; I could leave everything behind and just disappear."

"How different do you imagine your life in Dubai could be?"

Claudio does not respond instantly. His dark, velvety eyes become dreamy. "I would be respected ... looked up to ..."

This childish fantasy of power, to be '*il capo*' – the boss – permeates his desires: with young and vulnerable women from the East or with dependable foreign workers in Dubai, he can finally imagine enjoying a position close to absolute power.

"Claudio, but as I understand it, you are the boss of your own studio, so technically you are already '*il capo*', aren't you?" I am trying to bring him back to Earth, where things are far from being bad.

"I am," he nods, but looks unconvinced.

"But ...?"

"This is my father's studio. I inherited his name, his clients, even his secretary ..." Maria, the ageless assistant, knows the intricacies of the family business better than Claudio himself. Those two older women, holy-mother and Maria-the-secretary, seem to retain the power so relinquished by Claudio. They have disliked each other since the time Claudio's father was at the centre of their small claustrophobic stage.

"What kind of relationship did you have with your father?"

Claudio's face suddenly freezes, with a layer of ice so thick that I cannot even see his emotions.

"I admired him," he finally utters.

"Were you close to each other?"

"He was forty-seven and at the peak of his career when I was born. My mother always made sure I didn't get in his way, or run around or make a noise when he was meeting clients or working on a project."

This is how Claudio grew up, surrounded by women, his mother and a long list of obedient maids. Their job was to make sure the boy was kept at bay, well nourished and well behaved when his father would emerge from his studio to check on his drawings or his grades. His father reigned over a small kingdom: his wife, his maids, male and female employees all constantly seeking his approval, and fearing his judgement. Claudio desperately wanted to be just like him and, when the time arrived to choose a career path, he had no doubts and applied to architecture school. But he had not expected what he found out about his father's reputation from his peers: that of a ruthless competitor and a manipulator.

"Other students were wary around me, often envious, and sometimes curious. They never called me Claudio, for them I was just '*Il piccolo Fontana* – Fontana-the-little'." The label 'little' stayed with Claudio; despite his large frame, he continued to feel belittled.

Dropping his architecture studies did cross his mind a few times, but he was actually enjoying what he did, and had no other interests or inclinations. When he finally graduated, Claudio started applying to large international firms, in London and elsewhere, but his father died from a heart attack, so he had to promptly take over the family business.

"I am still working at his desk and sitting on his chair …," he adds, annoyed but still unable to recognise his own anger.

"Have you considered changing the furniture?"

"That would upset Maria … and *Mamma* would not be pleased …"

"So, you'd rather stay in your father's shadow, using whatever he left behind?"

"He had great taste by the way... invested in designer furniture … His desk is actually worth a fortune now." Claudio keeps selling me his father's impressive image.

"Do you worry about not being as tasteful if you change it?"

Claudio shrugs in a way that can be equally interpreted as a 'yes' or a 'no'.

At this point, I would not be surprised to learn that Fontana senior had passed on to his son an ageing mistress as well, one that Claudio could not change, for fear of ruining the excellent choice of his father. I imagine one of those Fellini-esque characters, plump, ageless and utterly sensual.

"I sent flowers to Eva." Claudio changes the subject for a more pleasant one. As usual, he illustrates his announcement with an image, which lands instantly into my chat box.

We both look at the same picture, a young woman holding a bunch of slightly faded roses, but what we see differs. On my side of the screen, Eva's revealing top made of a cheap shiny fabric, the full make-up of an anxious childish face and a slightly annoyed smile create an unsettling contrast with the presumed spontaneity of the scene – the shot is taken by the delivery man in the early morning. Claudio, for his part, is all eyes for her deep décolleté and her innocent blue eyes.

I force my imagination to slow down, to give Eva the benefit of the doubt – maybe she is a Cinderella looking for the right prince after all.

***

"Eva is so easy to please …"

This time Claudio starts with his favourite topic, making sure I do not try any other paths.

"So, unlike your father …"

"Why do you keep bringing him up? What does she have to do with him?!"

Now Claudio is unnerved. Hopefully I will not spend the rest of the hour looking at pictures of the potential bride.

"What would your father think about Eva, if you were to introduce her to him?"

"He is dead, remember?"

"Of course I remember. He is dead, but this does not automatically cancel him from the picture."

"Which picture are you talking about?" His voice is now trembling with rage.

"Your life. By the way, did he have affairs?" I am not sure where that question has come from, but I really want to shake Claudio and lure him away from his imaginary world of exotic brides.

"Why do you need to know?" he growls.

"Because he is still messing with your life, and I am trying to understand why you are letting that happen."

He calms down, all of a sudden not angry anymore.

"I always wondered … It wouldn't be unlike him. He craved admiration, and my mother did not give him enough of that. And he was also very good at hiding his tracks. When I was old enough to ride my own Vespa, I followed him a few times …" Claudio grows silent, lost in his teenage memories. As he resumes his tale, his expressive face is animated and his hands come to life in front of my screen. "He was difficult to shadow. He had a driver who drove him from one appointment to another … My father loved expensive hotels, and I soon discovered all his favourite spots, from Harry's Bar on via Veneto to Canova on Piazza del Popolo …"

Claudio took this detective game seriously; it kept him busy most afternoons for a whole school year.

"I got really good at it. I almost considered becoming a private detective."

"What were you hoping to find?"

"I don't know … something reckless, I guess …"

"Did you find anything?"

"Not much. I mostly saw him talking with some expensively dressed men, smoking cigars, and drinking endless Bellinis … It all looked rather boring … Until one day, when I caught him with a woman."

The way he pronounces 'una donna' – a woman – leaves no space for interpretation; he sounds hurt, but I can also hear admiration and envy.

"What kind of woman?"

"Blonde. Tall. The exact type that makes men turn their heads when she enters the room. Her mere presence put them at the centre of attention. He clearly enjoyed that. I still remember their laughter … her burgundy dress and long sparkly earrings …"

Claudio spied on them from outside Harry's Bar. His father was totally absorbed by his conversation. As they finally left the bar, laughing together at something his father had said, they jumped into a taxi (his driver had been discharged from his duties that day). Claudio tried to follow them with his *motorino* but lost them to the traffic, his frenetic race stopped on the riverbanks by a red light.

"Regrettably I did not find out for sure where he was taking her …"

"What was in your imagination?"

"Maybe a hotel … or perhaps he was renting her one of those chic tiny apartments that all powerful men seemed to arrange for their mistresses back then."

"Did you ever confront him about it?"

"That evening I tried to ask about his day, but he dismissed me with something nebulous about meeting with clients."

"So, after all, she could have been a client of his?"

"Are you joking? I saw them. Even through the thick glass of the window, I could see the sparks flying." His hand makes a gesture illustrating the sexual tension between his father and his mysterious lover.

After the death of his father, years after the Harry's Bar encounter, Claudio inherited some rented properties. One of them, a small terraced apartment just around the corner from Piazza Navona, was unoccupied. Claudio went to visit the place with an estate agent to arrange its sale.

"When I opened the door, I instantly guessed. This must have been the place she lived in."

The flat was empty, but everything about it screamed of her – a forgotten Chanel perfume bottle on the bathroom sink, with some golden liquid left at the bottom; the dark burgundy wall in the bedroom where the mark from a king size bed was still visible on the thick carpet …

"I just knew I could not sell this place."

He asked the agent to leave him alone and then explained to his mother that the place had to be refurbished to sell it at a better price. He kept the key, and up until now, he has resisted putting it on the market.

"Now I may use it for Eva … when she can come."

"Have you been fantasising about bringing a woman there for a long time?"

He nods almost invisibly.

The place, which he has kept away from his mother, has actually stayed unchanged, frozen in time, as a perfect container for his juvenile fantasies. He did not try to find out more about the former tenant, and sometimes he goes there to spend an hour sitting on the terrace, daydreaming about his father's secret life.

"I imagine that this was the place where my father made love many times, a place where he was probably talkative, charming, even passionate ..."

"Claudio, this lover of your father, we do not know that for sure but at least she clearly exists in your imagination ... Could she have something to do with the lack of concrete romantic partners in your life?"

He frowns and stares at me silently.

"Your father was a powerful presence in your life. When you saw this glamorous woman, whom you imagined as his lover, your self-confidence took another blow."

"For sure, no girls around me had anything in common with that woman, unfortunately."

"Claudio, this alluring woman may have existed in your imagination only," I say gently, very aware of breaking something precious.

"I saw her and she was beautiful," he defends his vision stubbornly.

"You did see her once when you were sixteen. She certainly was blonde, tall and elegant, but the mysterious lover that you have created based on those characteristics is an idealised version of her. You had so little information that your mind kept filling the gaps, attributing more and more details to her, which turned her into an unattainable vision."

Claudio looks confused: "So what?"

"I have the impression that as you try to find a romantic partner online, you are re-creating the same situation, in which there is no real woman but only gaps to fill with the bits of juvenile fantasies that you have kept and built upon."

He keeps looking at me, confusion mounting in his dark eyes.

"What do you mean by 'no real woman'? What about Eva, isn't she real?"

"She certainly is, but the online version of her that you have access to is an object of desire created artificially by the dating website and your own imagination."

"But I can travel there and meet her, to find out more." He keeps defending his dream.

"Can you really?"

"No, right now I can't. Damn it!"

Claudio is used to living around phantoms – the malignant ghost of his grandiose father, his mother reduced to the image of a saint as dictated by society and the glittery fantasy of his father's glamorous lover, seen only once briefly. As I look at Claudio's lonely face on my screen, I realise how cumbersome these phantoms have been. We have to get rid of them, in order to create some space in his life for more genuine relationships.

"Claudio, what about picking up that detective game of yours and pushing your enquiry a little further?"

"What do you mean?"

"Could you try to learn more about the person who rented this apartment?"

My hope is that replacing his father's imaginary lover with a more realistic version could help Claudio to break free from his juvenile fantasy.

"I can try," he agrees, not overly excited about the idea.

When we disconnect, I think about the mysterious blonde,

wrapped in the layers of Claudio's dreams. Who was she? Is she still alive?

As I write up my notes, the scene in Harry's Bar plays out in my mind as an Italian movie I have just watched. The teenager spying on his father stands out in the cold, looking at the lovers sipping on their Bellinis, their hands touching. He is feeling left out, not worthy of taking part in this brighter, exciting life that his father is living away from home. This is when he turns them into idols. Years later, they are still around and their presence constantly reminds him of his insignificance. 'A weirdo …,' his voice resonates in my head. I write down all of this, hoping that somehow, as Claudio's story takes shape, I am getting closer to helping him out from this lonely impasse.

***

"It can't be her," Claudio declares, his voice soaked with reproach.

"Really? Tell me more," I plead, but just by looking at his face I can tell that the spell is broken.

After our previous session, he went to 'her apartment' again. This time he asked the building's concierge about his father's old tenant.

"He had this smirk when I asked about her … I could tell he knew something." The concierge did not know much about her whereabouts, but added that she was friendly with the woman living next door, who may have her new address.

"It felt kind of exciting again, to chase her," Claudio recognises with a boyish smile.

He then drove to the address given by the neighbour, located near Rome. He parked his car in front of a small villa painted in pink and waited for an hour, until the front door was eventually opened and a woman started walking up the street, dragging a shopping trolley with a visible effort.

"She was nothing like the woman I had seen with my father. She was tall, her hair was dyed blonde, she was plainly dressed, without any sophistication. It just could not be her."

He looked at her walking down the street, and could not decide whether to leave his car to follow her and ask if she knew his father.

"Could it be her, a few years later, after all?"

"It probably could," he sighs.

We have not found out whether this lady was the secret lover of his father, out of the tailor-made stories from Claudio's imagination, but somehow the glamorous lover's image has been tarnished by the possibility of a real woman. The magic has gone, and as I listen to Claudio's tale, I feel some remorse for making this happen.

"I may sell this place after all, it costs a fortune," Claudio admits grudgingly. "It needs a lot of work and Eva deserves better. I told her I would come as soon as the borders open up, but I am not sure she was happy," he recognises, letting his anxiety take over.

"What do you think, what is going on for her?" I ask, giving his imaginary girlfriend another chance.

"I don't know … Maybe she is embarrassed about her life there?"

"And what about you? How would you feel about meeting her in the flesh?"

Claudio does not respond for some time; he seems confused.

"I want to go, but I am also scared that she may not like me," he finally utters, staring at me – a desperate call for reassurance. I have to fight my natural temptation to give him what he craves for and tell him that there is no reason she would not like him. There are actually many reasons for a young girl like Eva not to be attracted by a middle-aged, eternal bachelor like Claudio. I do not want to lie to him, so I keep silent and wait for more.

"I feel like a creep," he continues honestly. "I am thirty-nine and have never been in any kind of romantic relationship. How can I tell this to anybody without embarrassment?"

"You have just told me, haven't you?"

He shrugs, which I interpret as a not-very-flattering 'well, you are not really a woman'.

"Is this one of the reasons why you have been avoiding women who could be interested in getting closer to you?"

"I don't know. Maybe … I am turning forty next year," he adds, "and if I don't meet somebody before then, I will probably just give up."

"Let's make sure you do not." I make an offer I am not sure I can deliver on.

***

Claudio dials in from the park again, but this time it is raining, so unlike the Roman weather. Despite the black umbrella he is holding above his head, the hoodie he is wearing is soaked and he shivers.

"Won't you get wet sitting outside for an hour?"

"I am fine. I like the rain, actually."

For the first time Claudio does not jump in with some news about his imaginary online dating. We stay in silence and the sound of the rain falling invades our shared space.

"Is there something you want to tell me?" I break this increasingly heavy silence. With Claudio out there in the rain, I struggle to just sit and wait for him to volunteer something.

"At the end of this park is my school," he nods.

Claudio is staring at something above his smartphone,

probably the real reason for us being in this park.

"It is a Jesuit school, a very prestigious one. My father went there too. He was very proud of it."

"How old were you when you went to this school?"

"From eight to sixteen."

"Is it where you played football?" I suddenly remember him mentioning this a few sessions ago.

"Yes it is. Actually, I hated it."

There is so much emotion in his last words that I am taken aback.

"With the lockdown, all schools are closed …," he says, and now I can tell that he has a plan, maybe an unconscious one.

"Do you want to show me your school?" I ask, knowing the answer.

Claudio stands up and starts walking across the park. The pine trees are moving away behind his back in a Fellini-esque tracking shot.

"Let's see if the hole in the fence is still there," he says, turning to the right.

We make it through the fence. Twenty years have passed but the opening used by the boys for their secret outings is still there. Claudio strides across the fields, then stops and turns the camera around to show me the school premises. The terracotta buildings look as ancient and as beautiful as one would expect from an old Jesuit school in Rome.

"It has not changed at all," Claudio says and resumes his tour. "Let me show you somewhere."

He silently takes me via video through the football field, his tense face washed by the rain.

At last, he stops, his eyes riveted by something I cannot see, just in front of him.

"Where are we?" I finally ask to break his stillness.

"The locker rooms," he utters but does not move an inch, his features as still as his body.

"Did something happen in there?"

"Can I sit here outside?" he asks for permission, somewhat childishly.

"Of course, you can. Do you feel safe there? Are you alone?"

He looks around obediently, nods, and sits down on the wet grass under another pine tree. I notice that the rain has stopped and the birds have resumed their chatter.

"How old were you when something happened to you in those locker rooms?"

"Thirteen," he says almost inaudibly and looks away.

"Do you want to tell me about it today?"

He remains silent for a long moment, but then eventually, his voice still small, tells me what he has been keeping inside for more than two decades.

"An older boy … he was very popular, suggested we take turns to … make love to each other. I really liked him and wanted to be his friend. So, I did. He went first, and once he came, he pushed me away and refused to let me take my turn. He pulled his pants back on and laughed …"

As he tells me about the abuse he experienced, I feel his shame and it is excruciating.

"He betrayed you and turned what you expected to be a friendly sexual encounter into sexual violence. I can only imagine how terrible this made you feel."

"I felt humiliated … but I accepted it, and … I was aroused," he recognises.

"Claudio, you were only thirteen and you liked this older boy. I understand why you accepted his offer. He coerced you into this sexual act, and then abused you," I say the painful truth.

'Adesso sei un froccio' – you are gay now – the older boy whispered before leaving the locker room. Claudio sat on the floor crushed by what had just happened; those last words of the popular boy resonating in his ears.

"Am I? Did this make me gay?" he kept wondering for years, watching himself constantly, fearing the worse. In his father's world, 'gay' stood for an insult.

When Claudio returned home that day, he felt sick and scared that his father might somehow find out about what had happened to him.

"My father always praised strong men. He took pride in being one ..."

"Of course, you could not tell him about the abuse," I make sure I utter the words that he has been avoiding for years. He cringes and covers his eyes.

"This is so pathetic," he howls.

"There is nothing pathetic about sexual abuse. This was traumatic, and I am sad that you had to cope with this alone at the time."

"Why did he do this to me?" Claudio is still grappling with the pain of the betrayal and abuse.

"Something was very wrong with him; maybe he was looking for somebody vulnerable to assert his power?"

"His father was a big name in the military, a general of some sort ... There was some gossip that he was beating his son," Claudio remembers.

"He probably grew up in a system in which he felt small and disempowered ... He was desperate to get rid of these feelings, to pass them onto somebody else," I suggest.

"Small and disempowered? He was tall, the best football player and one of the most popular boys in the school!"

"Appearances are often deceptive. Based on what he did to you, he was struggling with the same feelings of inadequacy that you are struggling with now."

"Sick bastard," he finally says bitterly.

"Fair enough description," I agree.

In an attempt to help him out of his regression to the shame of his teenage years, I bring up statistics: one in six men has had experience of sexual abuse; five in six never report it and, on average, it takes a man twenty-six years to report the traumatic events.

He looks at me with disbelief.

"I thought this only happened to morons like me," he says with a heartening honesty.

"No, unfortunately this happens to many people, no matter their gender or age," I confirm the sad truth.

***

"She made up the whole thing," the words Claudio spits out can barely contain his hurt and his anger. Despite being indoors, mirrored sunglasses conceal his eyes. Their surface reflects his screen with surprising clarity; I can see a double reflection of myself in the lenses.

"What happened?"

"She spilled out everything!" he continues his unfathomable rant.

"Claudio, let's take a deep breath. Why don't you take off those sunglasses and fill me in?"

He exhales loudly, but follows my suggestion and puts the glasses away. Relieved to see those two tiny reflections of me disappear, I can finally meet his eyes. They are even darker than usual, dry and sparking with indignation. Caught between the wall and the desk, his resemblance to a trapped, wounded animal is even more striking than usual.

"Her name is Oksana, not Eva, we talked over the phone for the first time after months of messaging," he announces in a rather dramatic tone.

The story that Claudio then recounts in one breathless long tirade is as shocking as it is unsurprising. Oksana, like many other girls, is employed by the dating agency as 'an online escort'. Her job consists in luring foreign men into flirty relationships, chatting with them as much as possible, asking them for gifts, flowers or even money.

"Why don't you meet somebody your own age in Italy? Italian women are very beautiful, like Monica Berlucci," she offered gently in a surprisingly flawless English.

"Well done, girl," I think to myself. I ask aloud: "Why do you think Oksana volunteered this information?"

"I don't know … Maybe she was just fed up with talking with me."

"She was ready to risk losing the income she probably needs, in order to warn you. Have you asked her why?"

"I did. She said she liked me and didn't want me to spend all my time and money on this scam," he acknowledges.

"Claudio, I know you are disappointed, but …"

"Why? Why do these kind of things always happen to me?" he interrupts, almost screaming at me.

"Claudio, unfortunate things happen to many people. It sounds like many other men have fallen into this trap. But Oksana decided to tell *you* about it. What this may mean is that she cared enough about you to avoid you more trouble."

"Cared enough? Are you joking?" he protests mildly.

"Did she tell a bit more about herself?"

"Not much. But I asked, and it was her in the photo, by the way," he adds, inadvertently revealing his own initial doubts about Eva's realness.

"Do you think you will talk again?"

"She offered to video call."

"And?"

"I don't know. What for? She has been lying to me all the way through …"

"But then she told you the truth as soon as she could speak to you outside the website chat," I observe.

"She is a really nice girl, I told you," he mumbles, with visible regret for her loss.

"She certainly sounds it, I hope you can learn a little more about her." I am hoping that Oksana will collaborate in dispelling Eva, the idealised alter ego she had to create for her own survival.

"Once the pandemic is over, I may go to Thailand," Claudio states half-jokingly.

For an instant I see a fast-forward, an image of his aged face on the screen, palm trees in the background, telling me endless stories about other girls, always younger and more unattainable …

"What do you make of her suggestion about dating locally?" I make the most of Oksana's advice now that we can use that obvious idea at last.

"It will not lead to anything …"

"Why do you have to be so pessimistic?" I repeat jokingly, using one of his own expressions.

"I don't know …"

"What might happen if you met somebody in Rome?"

He fidgets uneasily in his chair, a few drops of sweat now visible on his shiny forehead.

"It is getting damn hot here," he wriggles his large body out of his chair. "Let me open the window." He leaves me in front of a white wall.

"What scares you about the idea of meeting a woman in the flesh?" I ask bluntly when his flushed face reappears on my screen.

"I don't know. I just don't think I can," he concludes stubbornly.

Claudio's fear is overflowing the frame, in an emotional acqua alta – high tide – that I am trying to contain, but he does not seem to have any means of accessing it, his shame is keeping guard.

We have to face that shame before we can go any further.

"Claudio, when was the last time you had an intimate interaction with a woman in flesh?"

"Do we count prostitutes?" he asks defensively in response.

Claudio saw them from time to time, always in the same massage parlour on the other side of the city. It was always a neat transaction and he would always keep his eyes closed. He could not tell what the woman really looked like. He kept his clothes on. Each time, after leaving the tiny and hot room, he felt 'bad'.

"Claudio, what is the issue with exposing yourself naked?"

He looks cornered, his body trapped in the screen frame.

"They will think I am fat," he finally admits with a sudden sincerity.

"Do you think you are fat?"

"I am fat … always been that fat boy always mocked by other schoolboys …"

I would like to reassure Claudio and tell him that people of all body shapes can find love, but I also know that this will only be partly true. The shame he feels about his body is what stands in the way of him getting into intimate relationships, not the fat. Extra shame is harder to lose than extra kilos.

"Then have you tried to do something about your weight?"

"I tried to stop eating. It did not work."

As I watch the shadow of shame passing through his round face, the nickname 'Fontana-the-little' comes back to my mind. Could his putting on weight, making his body bigger, be a desperate attempt to make himself more visible? When I ask he shrugs, but this time I do not let him off the hook: "Something like Fontana-the-little being actually big?"

"So what, is it a crime?" he hisses, offended.

"No, wanting to exist is not a crime," I say gently. "And extra kilos are not the only way to have more weight in life."

This time he does not fight, but I am not sure he can find the strength to turn to action.

"My guess is that when you start feeling that you exist beyond your father's shadow, you may feel differently about your body."

I refrain from suggesting he sees a nutritionist or a personal trainer, even if this impasse makes me feel cornered – I am desperate to get him out of his messy apartment, out of his locked-down city, out of the protective layers of his fat.

After our session, my body screams out for a run. Since the beginning of the pandemic, I have put on weight – more hours in front of the computer and a few more drinks on weekday evenings. Those few extra kilos slow down my run along the flooded riverbanks, but in striking contrast with Claudio, who still weighs heavily on my mind, I enjoy being in my body.

***

For the next few weeks, I do not see Claudio. He cancels one session after another, using more or less credible pretexts. I am starting to wonder if I will ever see him again, when he finally shows up.

This time he sits on the sofa and behind him, for the very first time, I finally see his interior. The apartment is messy indeed, with various objects, from model planes to a collection of plastic Marilyn Monroe figures of all shapes and sizes, filling the space. The atmosphere is boyish and strangely energetic.

"Thank you for inviting me into your living room," I acknowledge the risk he is taking.

"It is fine, you must have seen worse," he shrugs, but I know that something has shifted. No baseball cap, no sunglasses reflecting my own image, nothing to hide behind.

"I saw Oksana, we video-called."

"Wow, tell me more!"

"She was … different," he struggles to find the right words.

She connected from her kitchen, wearing jeans and an over-sized T-shirt, no make-up. "This is my girlfriend, Lena," she announced first thing, and the girlfriend, a plump brunette slightly older than her showed up and waved hello. "She also works for … the dating website," she adds.

"Yes, I am a lesbian," she confirmed with an ironic smile, breaking any illusions Claudio might still have.

Claudio felt awkward, but soon Oksana made him relax, chatting freely about their plans.

Working as 'online escorts' has been their way to save enough money to move abroad to pursue their studies. Her English is actually more fluent than his.

"It is just easier and more credible if 'Eva' does not speak much English," she explained with a mischievous smile.

"You are a very kind man, Claudio," she assured him at the end. "Different from the usual dicks we have to deal with."

As he repeats her words, Claudio looks uneasy.

"How do you feel about her saying this?"

"Angry."

"Angry at Oksana?"

"Angry at the universe; the one girl who is not repulsed by me is a lesbian."

"Claudio, Oksana appreciates you for a reason. You are a decent and kind man. But how can any women discover that if you keep hiding behind your father's desk and your extra kilos?"

We end the session with this question mark floating in the air. Pushing Claudio towards change is exhausting me and resisting it tires Claudio as well.

***

The next time we meet, there is an unfamiliar background behind Claudio: bookcases filled with books and scale models, framed prints on the wall showing some modernist buildings.

"I came to the office," he comments. "I have not been here in weeks ..."

I am somehow relieved to see him out of his solitary confinement. Unshaven and swallowed by a soft, velvety sofa, he looks depressed, but the change of scenery brings some energy into our virtual room.

"All this seems so foreign now ...," he looks around with dismay. "I don't know what I am doing here."

The studio has been shut for months, its wealthy clients have fled to their houses on the coast and the employees are working remotely on the very few projects that are still afloat.

"I cannot believe I have been coming here every day for more than ten years ..."

Claudio shows me around, the space seems frozen in time, I can feel how modern and chic it must have looked thirty years ago. His father's office was conceived as a glorification of his work and his persona: massive furniture, colossal prints of his projects.

"All this ... is just not me," Claudio concludes as he wriggles out of the sofa. "The only spot I love here is the terrace – let me show you."

He walks through the studio, opens the huge glass door and takes us outside. The vast sunny views of the Roman roofs are simply breath-taking. Claudio looks around in silence. Locked-down Rome is nearly noiseless.

"The sky is so empty … without the planes," he finally utters and looks straight into the camera. "You were right, I have been hiding behind my father's back."

This is not exactly what I had said, but this is the first time I hear him taking some responsibility for his avoidance.

"Last night, I wasn't able to get to sleep for hours … When I finally fell sleep, I was woken by a nightmare. I am sure you will love it," he smiles.

"If you say so …"

"I was hiding under my father's desk … As a child, I actually never did, as I was not allowed into his study anyway … But in the dream I was stuck under the desk, the room was dark, and I had neither enough space to move nor enough air to breathe …" As he recounts the dream, his breathing gets faster. "I was trying to get out, but could not. I was stuck there, suffocating … I woke up sweaty and cold, breathless."

When he is done with the dream, we both stay silent for a while. Then he turns around, looks towards his father's studio.

"This morning, when I came here, still thinking about the dream, I went online and put up an ad to sell the desk. I am done with it."

As he steps back into the room, he does not return to the desk, but stands in the middle of the room. He looks around again, as if he was seeing the place for the first time.

"And what about you? Now that you have managed to get out?"

"I am probably ready to leave this place."

"I know you are," I confirm, relieved. "Do you have a plan?"

"I may …," he smiles enigmatically, but he is not ready to tell me more.

This is the first time we end without planning for the next session.

"I will let you know," he promises, and this time I am certain he will.

***

Several weeks later, Claudio has stopped popping up in my thoughts. I know he is out of his corner, and at this point I want to trust him with taking the lead. I resist writing to him to find out more. I leave him with the breathing space he has finally claimed for himself.

When his name appears in the long list of new emails in my mailbox, I click on it, anxious to hear his news.

The first thing I see is an attachment – a picture of Claudio and a dozen people alongside him, men and women, Latino and white, all wearing masks. Behind is a building side. This is the first time I've seen Claudio surrounded by other people. I realise how tall he actually is.

"I am in Brazil, we are building an emergency hospital," the short note explains. "The architect who was directing the works died from Covid. They needed somebody ready to fly there and take over – that was for me."

I look at the picture closely and feel a wave of pride for Claudio. The way they all stand close to each other speaks volumes about their shared purpose. A tiny woman, who stands at his right, does not look into the camera; her head is turned towards Claudio. Their bare arms are touching and, in this probably innocent touch, I see hope for his healing.

"I will keep in touch, when I am back," he signs off.

I do not think he will, but at this point it does not matter.

VIII

Elena

Jersey City, NJ

"Mummy is busy right now, sweetie!"
     These are the first words I hear from Elena, her anxious voice entering my room even before I can see her face on the screen. A faint trace of a Russian accent confirms what her name suggested – we come from the same place.

I sit in front of my computer, sensing the tension building up on the other side across the Atlantic, as the banging on the door and negotiations are delaying the start of our session. I listen to her hurried steps, her impatient voice imploring the child to go away, the sound of a door being locked.

"Sorry, I just can't get away," she moans, this time in a melodious Russian; she sounds like she was raised in Moscow.

As Elena's face finally appears on my screen, I am taken by surprise – her Asian features contrast with what I expected.

"I don't think I can do this anymore," she claims and stares at me, waiting for something I do not have on offer – a solution, advice or a way out?

"Please, tell me about yourself. Where are you from?" I ask, all ears, ready to hear a new intricate story, a new fascinating world.

"I was born in Kazakhstan and lived in Moscow before moving

to New York," she explains simply.

They have been locked down for a few months now – her American husband Luis, their five-year old daughter Sonia, and herself – in a two-bedroom apartment in Jersey City. Before the pandemic everything was running smoothly – Luis drove to the office every day, dropping Sonia off at the nursery on his way, while Elena would take a bus to attend her rehearsals.

"I am a cellist with the New York Philharmonic Orchestra," she nods at her imposing instrument in the corner of the bedroom – a third silent participant in our conversation.

Until the pandemic struck, Elena used to travel extensively with the orchestra, and her fellow musicians, especially those from the cello section, were her second family and her main reality. The lockdown forcefully moved her family from the fringes to the very heart of her existence.

"I used to be a cellist with a husband and a child. Now I am a married mum with a cello," she sighs.

"How does this make you feel?"

"Confused … Frustrated … Angry. Sometimes I would just like to run away," she shares her feelings without hesitation, her eyes riveted on me. "But there is nowhere to go," she adds. "For the time being, the Philharmonic is shut down."

"Is it where you would usually go, when feeling confused, frustrated or angry?"

She nods and smiles before this evidence.

"So how are you coping now?"

"I am not. I just lock myself in the bathroom, open the shower and scream … silently, of course, to avoid waking up my daughter or terrifying my husband."

"So, you basically just suck it up," I sum up.

"I guess I do," she admits.

Elena

With her dark, straight hair, her slanting eyes and the cello case on her back, Elena is accustomed to being mistaken for Chinese. Some Asian stereotypes fit well with her character: she is a hard-working, dedicated person and, until she had her daughter, she did not find it particularly upsetting. As an Asian, Elena was expected to excel in her music practice and she always did. But when Sonia started nursery, Elena was suddenly hit by an even heavier set of stereotypes: "They expect me to be a typical tiger mum … but I am not," she admits, almost apologetically.

She was not sure she'd wanted children when, a year into the relationship with Luis, she got pregnant. They took this decision together, not on a whim, but in a kind of fog, probably due to their being freshly in love and her hormones running wild.

"With Sonia I feel like a constant failure, I never seem to get it right," she complains. "She is difficult. She throws a tantrum every time I ask her to do something, like putting her pants on or putting her toys away … She just screams 'no', pushes me away, and cries in her room for hours!"

Her daughter does exactly what Elena herself is not allowed to do, she expresses her frustration loudly, protests against the imposed activities or the current lockdown restrictions (not playing with her friends at the nursery, not being allowed to enjoy her favourite playground).

"I have never been particularly patient with her, but now … Sometimes I worry I might even hurt her."

"Have you ever done so?"

"Of course not."

"It is natural to lose patience with young children, especially now when you are under constant stress and thinly stretched," I make an attempt at normalising what feels abnormal to Elena.

"This is not what Luis' mother says," she utters bitterly.

Her mother-in-law lives just a twenty-minute drive away and loves spending time with her granddaughter. Before the lockdown, she particularly enjoyed paying random visits, which Elena used in order to go out or practise for her next concert, but now this has been replaced by long video calls, during which Elena tries to focus on something else, like cooking or cleaning, avoiding being caught on her husband's phone camera.

"And what about your mother?"

"Luckily she is not particularly interested in grand-parenting. She is a musician."

"Does one exclude the other?" I ask, but she does not reply, probably considering it a purely rhetorical question.

Elena's mother has always taught piano, first in Kazakhstan at a local music school, then giving private lessons when the family moved to Moscow. She passed her passion for music onto her daughter, giving her a first 1/8th cello when Elena was just five years old.

"My mother kept it and just before Sonia's fifth birthday she sent it over for her to start taking lessons."

"And did Sonia start cello then?"

"Yes, but she is not interested at all."

The timing for starting music lessons could not have been worse. Elena found a teacher who came to their place a few times. At first Sonia seemed curious and accepting, holding the instrument and pulling the strings, following a simple rhythm. However, after a couple of lessons, when the teacher rang the doorbell, she sprinted to the bathroom, blocked the door with her little body, and Elena could not even get in.

"It was so embarrassing, the teacher was alone in the sitting room, waiting for us, and Sonia was blocking the door, just repeating 'no, no, no' in response to my attempts to get her out. I felt absolutely awful!"

For the last lesson, just before the lockdown, Elena tried to force the door, hurting her daughter in the process, not really badly, but enough for her crying to escalate. The teacher, who was also Russian, suggested, with a visible disapproval, postponing lessons to 'when the child is ready'.

The teacher uttered the word 'child' with a face mixed with disgust and disappointment.

"Exactly the same face my mother would make at any small mistake I made when learning a new piece," Elena adds. "With her perfect pitch, she was totally distressed by each and every one of my early musical blunders. "So, just to avoid seeing that expression on her face, I practised for hours. Or sometimes that wouldn't be enough, and then I would simply avoid looking at her, which made her go completely nuts."

As the cello teacher left, with Sonia hysterical in the bathroom, Elena knew that she would not come back. She was in high demand, especially among Russian circles in New Jersey, and had no time to deal with capricious pupils.

"Now I am dreading the prospect of having to teach Sonia myself," Elena says and stays silent, considering the consequences of this potential calamity. "My mother taught me at the beginning … I do not remember much of it, but she always said that it was a disaster. I was uncooperative and stubborn. Hiring a teacher saved her nerves and my life," she concludes, mimicking her mother's sarcastic tone. Her eyes drift away from the camera. Her mother, now thousands of miles away, still has the power to make Elena feel ashamed.

"How is your present relationship with her?" I take the risk of asking, knowing already that the few minutes that remain in our session will not be enough to start finding answers to this question.

"Bad," Elena states simply, and the expression of her face

colours this monosyllabic word with all the intricate and painful nuances that it cannot convey.

***

"I always imagined that, one day, I would sit in front of a therapist and talk about my mother," Elena begins exactly where we had left off. "And now, here I am ... but I am not sure where to start, what to say ... It feels like I have nothing to complain about, some of my friends have had it badly, but I was fortunate I had a hard-working and extremely supportive mother."

Elena connects from the same bedroom I saw her the first time; her cello standing guard in the same corner. She stays silent for a long moment, her eyes looking away from the screen, possibly at some window I cannot see. When she finally turns back, her lips move, but no words come out. She gazes at me in distress, unable to utter a sound.

"And what were you saying to that imaginary therapist?"

"I actually spoke English with him ..."

"Would you find it easier to switch to English to talk about your mother?"

She nods with relief, and the English words finally flow out.

"I always knew I was blessed with an amazing mother ... She has always been present, sending messages after every important concert, congratulating me with every new recording."

But actually, her mother's compliments made Elena cringe and what she felt was closer to shame than to pride. This 'inappropriate' reaction confirmed to her mother how ungrateful a daughter Elena was indeed.

"You never really had the patience to teach me anything," Elena wanted to protest at times, but she did not dare to. Her mother's narrative about her parenting was cast in stone; Elena therefore doubts her own memories. All the more so as there has never been anybody close enough to their double act to do a reality check – no siblings, no grandparents, no men.

"And what about your father?" I query, feeling slightly claustrophobic about the bubble in which Elena and her mother seemed to evolve.

"They parted when I was a baby, my mother did not want to see him ever again. When she returned to Moscow, pregnant, he stayed in Kazakhstan. She always said that we were better off without him anyway," Elena adds bitterly. "She always did everything for me. Paid for my cello lessons, took me to concerts all the time. We were like a team of athletes, running for my musical accomplishment. And now that I have succeeded, somehow I constantly feel guilty."

"Guilty? For what reason?"

"For leaving her behind, I guess? But then, she never wanted to emigrate … She would not leave her students. She has never learnt English either, which excludes her from moving here. I constantly feel that I am a bad daughter and a bad mother – this is a lot of failure for one single person."

"Your mother sounds very ambitious," I observe.

"Oh, she is rather selfless. She always assures me that she is satisfied with her teaching. She keeps repeating that I am the one with real talent in our family."

Her mother's self-effacing behaviour conceals her disillusion with her own low-key musical career. She craves for what her daughter managed to achieve – living abroad, travelling the world and playing for one of the world's most prestigious orchestras.

"I have never managed to produce a soloist," Elena's mother lets drop in one of their conversations, when Elena, as too often, tries to reassure her about her professional value. This sentence gets stuck in Elena's mind, confirming an already deeply seeded shame: her mother wished she had turned out to be an even more accomplished musician. She tries to brush it away, not to take it personally, but her mother has kept feeding her self-doubt in many more or less subtle ways.

"Oh come on, you are not a soloist," she said once, as Elena was complaining about the lack of time to practise.

"That is harsh," I sympathise. "It sounds like your mother expects an awful lot from you."

"A real tiger mum," Elena confirms, with bitter sarcasm.

Suddenly, only halfway through our session, the sound of banging on the door makes Elena jump. She turns away from the camera and a little girl in bright blue pyjamas jumps in.

"Mummy, I spoiled it all!" she complains in a high-pitched voice and she puts a drawing and her crayons in front of Elena. "Please, help me draw this kitten!"

"Sonia, I am busy," Elena switches back to Russian.

"But you are not playing, are you?" Sonia responds with steely logic, in English, and climbs on her mother's lap. Tears of frustration are already drying on her round cheeks; her auburn hair is tied up in two symmetrical bunches. She finally looks at the screen and discovers my presence. Shy, she hides her face on her mother's chest, forcing Elena to smile apologetically.

"Hi, Sonia," I say gently. "How do you do?"

"This is Anastasia, we work together," Elena explains to her daughter.

The little girl finally looks at me with her bright dark eyes and announces stubbornly in English: "I don't want to be a musician."

Elena's jaw visibly drops.

"And who do you want to be?" I surrender and continue in English.

"A doctor," she responds very seriously.

166

"Why a doctor?"

"Because I don't want everybody to die," she says and starts doodling something, her attention already on to the next thing.

"Sorry about this," Elena switches back to Russian. "There is no way for her to entertain herself for more than an hour."

"She is a very smart young person," I comment.

"She is," Elena sighs. "I cannot believe what she just told you … She probably thought you were also a music teacher. The only people I speak Russian with these days are my mother and the cello teacher she hated."

Our conversation is an illustrative example of the bilingual hurdle they both live with. Sofia is unwilling to speak Russian and prefers responding in English, which Elena takes as another confirmation of her bad parenting.

"I am sorry about this," Elena repeats her apology, with Sonia refusing to leave her lap. "Maybe we should end earlier today."

"Mummy, I'm hungry." Sonia gladly confirms that the session is over.

***

Elena's place in her family is a familiar one for me – I am also caught between a child, whose mother tongue is different from mine, and a mother who has not mastered the language that I speak most of the time. As an emigrant, Elena has to constantly play the interpreter; every time her mother tries to engage with her daughter, Elena has to translate. How does this situation shape their relationship?

That evening, I am still pondering this question, when my parents call for our usual video chat. As an emigrant, I have used technology for years to maintain my relationships, and with the pandemic grounding all flights between Paris and

Saint Petersburg, we have to rely on it even more heavily. As my teenage daughter hears my parents' remote Russian voices, she joins me in front of the screen. I observe their conversation closely. My daughter regresses quickly, as her Russian is not fluent enough to accommodate her current maturity. My parents adapt, following her into the playful childish mode – they make faces, add illustrative gestures to their words, and use paper and crayons to play games. They both had careers in fine arts and find it natural to use images to compensate for the gaps in their granddaughter's vocabulary.

As I listen to their joyous, patchy chat, Elena and her mother keep returning to my mind. Artistic language, be it music or fine arts, can be a wonderful way to communicate our deeper emotional states, but in intimate relationships can it replace all words without taking something crucial away?

**

As Elena picks up the call for our next session, I can hear a romantic cello tune with its powerful streams of complex emotions, but as the image comes in, I see Elena sitting in front of her camera, her instrument standing patiently in the corner, as usual.

"I recorded my practice yesterday," she explains with a smile. "It's the only way to keep my daughter outside this room."

Sonia learnt early that when her mother is practising her cello, she must not be disturbed. This rule is the only one she has accepted easily; in exactly the same way Elena-child respected her mother's sacred moments of piano playing. She always knew that her students and the instrument came first. She got used to being second.

Their Moscow flat consisted of two different sized rooms and a tiny kitchen. In the larger room, her mother gave private piano lessons, mostly in the evenings and weekends.

Elena was left with the smaller bedroom, in which they both slept, and with the kitchen, where she would heat up her meals alone and read books, trying to tune out the sound of the piano and her mother's authoritative voice whenever the student made a mistake.

"I remember, when I was young, sitting in the corridor for hours in front of the piano room door. I was often hungry and sometimes, at the end of the lesson, my mother would find me asleep on the floor in the corridor …"

At some point her mother realised that Elena had absorbed most of her lessons on musical theory. She took pride in her daughter's talent, which became apparent when she was around six or seven. She often told stories about how she would find her little girl playing an entire piece on the piano as she had heard it practised by a student, without ever seeing the sheet music, all by ear.

"She learns faster than my teenage pupils," Elena would often hear her mother boasting in front of her colleagues from the music school. Those words would fill her with pride but also anxiety, as deep down she doubted her own capabilities.

"I constantly felt in competition with her students, their invisible presence taking over everything we did. I never saw them, but I knew their names, recognised their fearful voices and the pieces they prepared for their next audition. My mother was frustrated with several of them, spending all our dinners talking about their lack of progress, their technical shortcomings and her hopes for their future, but mainly their failures. I knew I had to do better than each of them …"

As Elena finished telling her story, the sound of her cello takes over. For a few seconds we both listen to its dramatic melody, a perfect soundtrack for her childhood spent in the shadow of her mother's dedication to teaching music. A fleeting shadow on Elena's face indicates that she is dissatisfied with an imperfection in her playing.

"How did you choose to become a musician?" I ask, her daughter's rebellious voice still resonating in my mind.

"I didn't," she admits. "I always knew that this is what I would eventually do."

Music was at the very centre of their small world, leaving Elena with limited space for any other dreams.

"And why the cello?"

"Oh, this is the only time I rebelled," she smiles. "When the time came for me to enrol at the music school, around the age of seven, my mother presumed I would go for the piano, which I could play better than many other 'talented' kids. She was proud of my performance. But the day of the audition, when they asked me which instrument I would like to play, I said 'cello'. My mother was not allowed in the room, so she didn't know about it until the admissions lists were made public."

"You hadn't told her about your choice?"

"How could I? I was too scared of her reaction. I had no idea what she thought about the cello. Based on her random comments, I knew that not all instruments were equal … and their ranking affected the musicians who played them. I kind of guessed violin would probably be OK, but cello seemed beyond her radar. It was also different enough from the piano, but big, imposing and loud enough to compete with it. I am now surprised I didn't go for the contrabass," she smiles dreamily.

As they were standing in front of the list of children admitted to the music school, her mother was holding her hand and frantically reading the names of the chosen ones, put on the path to eventually becoming professional musicians. Elena clearly remembers her mother's fingers squeezing hers the moment she spotted her name on the list. But a few seconds later, she realised that it was in the strings department, under the 'cello' section. She squeezed Elena's hand even tighter, then looked at her in disbelief.

"I still remember that look of hers ... I could not decipher it; I just knew I had done something terribly wrong."

Elena choosing a different instrument meant that her mother could not teach her anymore. They continued their piano lessons, but this soon became secondary, and Elena's energy went totally into the cello, and away from her mother. Their tight bubble had been shaken.

It took her mother a long time to forgive Elena for what she saw as a betrayal. For a few months she was reluctant to take an interest in her practice or compliment her on her progress which was initially slow but soon became remarkable. Elena threw herself into this new challenge with all the ardour and dedication she was capable of. Soon excellent grades and her teacher's praise started to pour in. This is when her mother's tone became softer and she eventually stopped calling Elena's cello a 'behemoth'.

"It is rather interesting that Sonia is now rejecting your instrument in the same way you rejected your mother's years ago," I observe quizzically.

"At least, she did not come up with playing percussion ... Well, not yet!" she answers with irony, but her eyes are in turmoil. "Do you mean that I am the same as my mother?"

"What do you mean by 'the same'?"

"I don't know ... Not letting my daughter make her own choices freely?"

"Do you feel that becoming a musician was not your choice?"

She stays silent, considering my question at length.

"I don't really know. I never saw it as a choice," she admits.

"Your daughter does though. This probably means that you did something differently from your mother, allowing her to rebel," I respond.

From her look I can see that she does not believe me easily, of course, but this time she does not argue.

***

Our new session begins with the cello recording again playing in the background.

"Something weird has happened," Elena whispers, her face close to the camera. I have to increase the volume on my computer to distinguish her words. The music intensifies accordingly, covering the sound of her voice.

"My mother-in-law phoned a few days ago," she announces before pausing. "She called on my mobile when Luis was out on a walk around the block with Sonia. I tried to wriggle out of the conversation, but she insisted we had to talk 'seriously'. Coming from her, this 'seriously' freaked me out. I thought she had cancer or something ..."

"And?"

"She was calling to warn me that if I didn't change my behaviour, I might lose her son."

Elena had never had a proper conversation with her mother-in-law, beyond discussing trivial and logistical issues, mostly related to Sonia. Elena emerged shaken, not knowing what to make of that warning. She had never questioned her marriage. Luis had seemed to accept gracefully her passion for music.

"Does Luis know about his mother's call?"

"No, she insisted it was her initiative ..."

"What did she mean by the 'behaviour' that you should change?"

"She said something about me never being there, not caring

for him or my daughter … But I am stuck here all the time!"

"You are … But does Luis himself complain about anything?"

"No, not really. He always loved music but never played an instrument himself. He can't even sing in tune, but often jokes that marrying a musician has enabled him to sneak into the world of music."

"Could your marital problems just be in your mother-in-law's imagination?"

"I don't think so. She has no imagination …," she jokes and then wonders, staring at me in disbelief. "Is he having an affair?"

"Is that what your mother-in-law said?"

"No, but … she alluded to the possibility."

"And what do you think?"

"I never thought about it …"

Since that call, Elena has been watching her husband closely, without being able to discern any sign of emotional turmoil; his demeanour is calm and even, as usual.

"Is he seeing somebody?" she keeps wondering, increasingly distressed.

"How can I know?" I respond honestly. "What about asking him directly?"

Elena shakes her head vehemently.

"Why not?"

"I don't know … It will look stupid."

"Is it stupid to discuss your relationship with your husband?"

"I don't know … We never talk about the two of us," she admits. "The last time we did was when I got pregnant."

"So, he may be entirely dissatisfied with your marriage, considering a divorce or having an affair, and you wouldn't guess?"

She shrugs, letting the cello take over, as usual.

"What do you talk about at the dinner table?"

"We did not have that many dinners together before ... I would usually grab something on my way to the Philharmonic and he would feed Sonia."

But now, with the lockdown, they eat their meals together. Elena does all the talking, narrating the never-ending orchestra anecdotes to Luis, who listens with interest without interrupting or showing impatience.

"What kind of job does he do?" I realise that after several hours spent with Elena, I still have no idea about her husband's occupation.

"He works for a bank," she answers. "I can't explain what exactly ... I have always found it terribly boring."

Anything outside the musical world seems foreign and slightly surreal to her.

"But you chose to marry a non-musician, didn't you?"

"I did," she nods. "Maybe I wanted something different."

For a long time, Elena could not decide to tell her mother about Luis. She only called her when she became pregnant with Sonia and announced the changes to come.

"What was her reaction?"

"She stayed silent for a long minute ... We were not on a video call, but I could picture her face exactly. Then she congratulated me dryly and changed the subject to some concert she had attended"

Elena had intuited her mother's disapproval of her choice; Luis was not a conductor or a famous soloist after all.

"She had high hopes for you in this area as well ..."

"She had ... and I knew I had disappointed her again," Elena sighs.

"You have learned to discern your mother's disappointments very well ... But what about you? How do *you* feel about your choice?"

"Pretty content, I guess," she responds but looks unconvinced.

"You guess?"

"I used to be happy … before all this pandemic came and turned everything upside down," Elena responds angrily.

"Upside down? It sounds like the pandemic forced both your husband and your daughter from the fringes to the centre of your life, which was previously dominated by music."

Elena nods. A relationship in which music is not at the centre is alien to her indeed. Her earliest relational bubble consisted of her mother, herself and their instruments. It was a model in which music always took precedence, and only through their shared passion were they able to connect together.

"Being pushed to the margins … Does it sound familiar?"

Elena looks at me in dismay, unsure about the meaning of my question.

"When you talk about your early childhood, I have the impression that not only your mother's piano took all the space in your flat, but it also pushed you to the margins of your mother's world," I share honestly what has been on my mind for a while.

"Do you mean that I am doing the same to Luis and Sonia that my mother did to me?"

It is my turn to nod silently. As I am looking at her distraught face, the little Elena is with us again. She is sitting in a dark corridor, her back against the tightly closed door; behind her the piano is playing dramatically. In her solitude, she listens to the music, her lips mimicking the melody. She is trying hard to remember the piece to impress her mother later, desperately hoping for a place in her world.

"How did you feel when you were sitting outside your mother's door?" I ask.

"Lonely … unimportant … as if I didn't really exist …" she answers, tears in her eyes, "at least, not for her, not at that moment."

"Do you think your husband may feel this way sometimes?"

My question takes her off-guard; she stares at me in bewilderment. "I have no idea, really ... But why are you asking?"

"You know, we have been talking for a while now, and I still have no sense of what kind of a person your husband is. His presence in your life seems a little ghostly," I say, bringing us back to her present world. "So, when you say that as a child you used to feel 'as if you didn't really exist', I wonder whether unconsciously you may make Luis feel the same."

"How would I do this?" she asks defiantly as her face goes blank.

"By keeping him on the margins, not talking with him about anything deeply personal, by not letting him into your world, which seems mainly occupied by your work at the Philharmonic ..." I suggest.

" ... Just like my mother," she finishes my sentence and sighs.

"And you had nobody else in your life back then to make you feel more real, to place you at the centre of their life."

She hides her eyes from the camera. "No ... I was really alone and desperate for a pet, a dog or a cat, anything living really ... I kept imagining its warm, furry body on my lap, as I sat on that floor. I thought that if only I had a dog, I would never be alone any more ... but my mother absolutely refused. She disliked animals and was afraid a pet would distract me from music."

As she tells me about her longing for a pet to make up for her mother's misplaced love, my own daughter pops readily into my mind. She has been obsessed with the idea of having a dog, even before the pandemic. Together with my husband, we have been standing strong, for the sake of our freedom and the chance of sleeping in on Sundays, slowly reclaimed as she grew older. I suddenly feel a pang of guilt – have we been simply selfish?

"... And you will love this ..." Elena adds making me instantly return from wandering off to questions about my own life.

Each time I hear this from my client, I feel blessed – something clicking into place, between our conversations and their current life events.

"Sonia has been nagging us about having a cat since the beginning of the pandemic. One of her friends at school has got a kitten, and now she is completely obsessed with the idea. She keeps drawing cats, talking about cats ... It is completely insane."

"And how do you feel about having a pet now?"

"Until we spoke today, I completely forgot about ever wanting a pet. I guess it was just a stage, and then it passed ... Maybe it will pass for Sonia as well?"

"It may. But what do you make of this obsession of hers?"

"Nothing. All kids ask for a pet at some point, don't they?"

"They do, and it does not automatically mean that they are lonely or missing their mother's attention," I respond, probably reassuring myself more than Elena.

When we finally hang up, no matter how much I usually enjoy Bach, my ears are bursting; I have had enough. During the session I did my best to filter off the instrument and focus on Elena's words and feelings. As a result, I feel mildly irritated and headachy ... and surprise myself by feeling resentful towards her cello. During the session it was keeping me at bay, at a distance from Elena. Is it how Elena-child felt about her mother's piano? Is it something Sonia may also feel at times? This could explain her stubborn refusal to play an instrument ...

I leave my office and join my family in the sitting room. My husband is at the piano, improvising some jazz tune. My daughter is doing her best to follow the melody with her newly acquired ukulele.

"This will be a long evening," I think and retreat to my bedroom.

***

"We had an argument. First time ever," Elena announces reproachfully when we reconnect.

I had been mentally preparing for another session with some cello playing in the background, so the silence surrounding her this time is surprising.

"Luis has taken Sonia to see his mother. They are in the park." She explains the unusual absence of music and continues: "When I told him about his mother's call, he got upset but ended up spilling it all out."

Everything Elena had believed about her marriage was shaken instantly: "He claims he has always felt left out and unworthy of my attention."

"And you do the same to Sonia," he dropped as a final blow to her parenting. "Your own daughter complains that you love your cello more than her."

"Is that true?" I ask.

Elena stays still and silent, long enough for me to start wondering whether the connection is lost and the image has frozen. When she finally responds, her voice is thin and childish: "Maybe … I hate to think this, but … I cannot imagine myself surviving without my instrument … and I know I would be perfectly fine without Luis or even without Sonia …"

She looks at me upset by her own words. "This is such a terrible thing to say about your own child."

I am more touched by her shame than by her words. As a parent, I instantly resonate with the guilt she feels about her maternal limitations.

"Many women feel this way at times … and trying to

simultaneously be a good musician and a good mother is hard work," I say, doing my best to reassure her. My own mother comes to my mind; her passion for teaching art weighed more than parenting for her. The child in me is still hurt and wants to scream in resentment, punishing Elena. I have to gently put the neglected child aside and step back into my adult therapist's shoes.

"I am not sure you can understand," Elena blurts before I can add anything. She stares at me in confusion.

"Is that because I am not a musician?"

She nods in agreement and we stay silent together, listening to the sound of rain against our respective windows, in a strange synchronicity across the Atlantic.

"I mean, I do feel that you understand me though ... Sometimes I realise that you know me better than anybody else, but ... there is always this part of me that you cannot see, that remains outside of this," she makes an inclusive gesture to describe therapy.

"Do you feel the same way about Luis?"

"I do," she admits sadly.

"And what about your friends from the orchestra? Do they have access to this hidden part of you?"

She shakes her head with a desolate smile: "No, they are all too busy with their own music ..."

"Just like your mother ... which makes your world a rather lonely place," I say, and tears come to her eyes.

"And what happens when you are playing for an audience?"

"I feel less lonely ... I feel they share all my doubts and hidden truths. But as soon as the music ends, that feeling goes."

"And you are lonely again. Would you like to play for me ...?"

At first Elena looks at me in bewilderment, then stands up and goes to her instrument, which has been patiently waiting in its corner. Then she takes her bow out of the case, settles on a stool and installs the curvy instrument between her legs. She does not glance at the camera, but I know that she is very aware of my presence. She closes her eyes for a long moment, then her arm moves, putting everything else into movement – the bow, her other hand on the strings, her face, the whole cello … I do not recognise the music she is playing, but it takes over our shared space, it takes over the sounds of New York and Paris, it takes over our fears and our doubts.

As she plays, I slowly discern her better, as if the little Elena was recovering her space, welcoming me into her lonely, enchanted world. In this moment I experience being really close to Elena, her music miraculously bridging our past and present realities.

When her cello grows silent, we remain quiet for another long moment. Elena slowly returns her instrument back on its stand, the bow into its case and comes back to her computer.

"Thank you for letting me get closer," I can finally utter. My own voice seems intrusive and irrelevant after the music.

"Thank you for insisting," she echoes simply, and we finally both smile in relief.

"Do you ever play for Luis in this way?"

"I used to … but not any more … He is often busy with Sonia when I practise, then she is asleep and I do not want to wake her up."

"Would you like to play for him again?"

"I am not even sure he is still interested. He may be seeing somebody … not a crazy musician this time …"

"The only way to dispel this doubt is to ask him directly," I suggest, surprised by her train of obsessive thoughts.

She does not promise anything, but agrees to think about it.

As we disconnect, her cello keeps resonating in my mind, and for a second I wonder whether it was a good idea to invite her to play. It was a way for us to get closer, but by letting her cello take over our interaction, we may have re-enacted her familiar theme: music at the centre stage, sweeping Elena to the background. This thought keeps worrying me until the following week …

***

"I spied on my husband," Elena tells me in lieu of a greeting.

I do not try to hide my surprise, which only mirrors her own.

"The other afternoon he said he would go for a walk after leaving Sonia with his mother. I don't know what possessed me. Without thinking I just followed him outside … I had to discover what he was up to."

Luis strode towards the river, turning at the different crossings without hesitation. He was clearly heading somewhere and Elena followed closely behind, her heart pounding heavily in her tight chest. She was not trying to conceal her chase, she almost wished he would notice her and explain it with a credible lie, but Luis was busy with his goal to get where his lover was certainly waiting for him. Now Elena was convinced she saw right through his little game.

After fifteen minutes of this tailing, Luis paused in front of a building on Hudson Street. He rang the intercom and was quickly let in. Elena narrowly avoided being run over by a bus as she rushed across the street. As she reached the glass door, Luis was gone, certainly up into his secret lover's apartment.

Elena stood there for a few minutes, looking at the long list of residents, not knowing exactly what to do next. When her eyes recovered their ability to see and her brain became clear again, she saw a sign under the bell – 'The true self therapy practice' – it announced proudly in flowery letters. She peered at her watch – it was exactly five pm.

"I suddenly felt so silly," she recognises. "He came out exactly fifty minutes later."

As Luis walked back home, she followed at a distance, too ashamed to approach him.

"Did he ever mention that he was seeing a therapist?" I ask, bemused.

"No, and I haven't told him I was seeing you either ...," she admits.

Later that evening, after Sonia was asleep, Elena finally found the courage to tell Luis about everything that had been happening in her locked-down world – from our weekly calls to her suspicions about him having an affair.

"As soon as I told him I was seeing a therapist, he said he had been talking to someone since before the pandemic."

"Why didn't you tell me?" she had asked indignantly.

"Maybe for the same reason you did not tell me!" he replied. "I thought you weren't interested, too busy with your rehearsals and concerts."

They argued quietly in the kitchen, hoping not to disturb their daughter, sleeping tightly, exhausted by the time spent outside with her grandmother.

"We screamed at each other, cried and ended up hugging ... I could tell he had been seeing a therapist," she smiles. "He spoke about his feelings as he had never done before ... I didn't even know he had all these feelings really," she adds.

During the confrontation, Luis brought up Sonia's dream of a cat as an example of how inattentive Elena was to her needs and desires.

"What is it all about? Do *you* want a cat?" she asked her husband.

"No, *I* don't. But Sonia does. Why don't we just put her needs first for once?"

At that point Elena could not argue any more. "I just felt like all my anger evaporated suddenly, and I felt sad for Sonia and her feeling lonely."

At that point a kitten just seemed like an obvious idea.

"Her birthday is coming up ...," she adds, "and we will not even be able to organise a party. So, we decided Sonia would get a kitten."

She sighs, and I am not sure whether it is out of regret or relief.

***

"Meet Do-re-mi, I am in charge of her today," she announces and holds a kitten in front of the camera for me to see. The feline stares at me with her round, bewildered eyes. Elena tenderly strokes its stripy fur and settles it back on her lap.

The kitten fiddles with the strings of Elena's hoodie, unaware of its own symbolic charge – its tiny warm body on Elena's lap is tangible proof that she is trying to provide her daughter with what she could not get from her own mother.

"I can see that you are getting along well," I comment, trying to go beyond the kitten's cuteness.

"You were right, I needed this little beast as much as Sonia did," she responds quickly, letting the kitten chew the strings. "Now I clearly remember how badly I wanted a pet ... And Sonia was so happy! Why wasn't my mother able to do this for me? Was it too much of a sacrifice?"

By attending to her daughter's needs, Elena recognises her own. She puts Sonia first, doing exactly what was unattainable for her mother. Her attempts to repair this earlier hurt results in an unavoidable confrontation with her mother.

"I told my mother about Do-re-mi, and she freaked out, exactly like she did when I brought a kitten home ... I was around nine or ten. I found it on the street, near our rubbish bins. It was tiny and barely alive from hunger and cold."

"You never mentioned this before …"

"No indeed … It was pretty awful. I had to return it to the street that same evening. She would not tolerate it at home even for a day. I cried my eyes out."

Now, again, her mother's reaction to the exciting news of a kitten for Sonia came as a major blow: "How foolish! Why would you take on such a burden?" her mother howled at Elena over Zoom.

"This is where I lost it. I felt absolutely furious and just blurted out everything …"

"So, what did you tell her?"

"That she had never put me first and I had been lonely while she was busy turning her students into musicians. That I want to be a better mother than she was. That Sonia is missing her friends, she is lonely and for once I want to put her first. 'But how can *you* understand this?' I remember shouting at the end."

Her mother smirked as usual, rejecting Elena's reality, too uncomfortable to accept what has been said. "How ungrateful of you. I sacrificed everything for you. And this is why you are where you are now."

"That doesn't sound very fair." I gladly add some fuel to the fire.

"Fair? Are you joking? What she really needed was for me to achieve what she could not achieve. She never asked me what I wanted or needed. And what I needed was love, if not from her, at least from a fucking cat," she bristles, her eyes sparkling with rage.

"This pandemic has really got to your head," her mother concluded with an infuriating coolness. Before she could hang up, Elena dropped her final nuke: "And Sonia is not taking cello lessons. She does not want to become a musician. She may change her mind, but right now she just wants a cat and she will have one."

"She probably thought I was completely out of my mind," Elena tells me.

"And what do *you* think?"

"I think that, on the contrary, I am slowly recovering it ..."

***

In another startling twist, once Sonia got her kitten, she talked about starting music lessons.

"She told me that she actually likes the piano, so we borrowed a beginner's Clavinova from friends," Elena shares, with barely hidden excitement.

In an ironic way, Elena's story is circling back to its very roots.

"How do you feel about her choice?"

"It's rather strange ... but I am actually glad," she acknowledges. "I announced this to my mother when she called again. She was absolutely thrilled. And right now they are playing piano together via Zoom in the other room," she glances towards the locked door. "I almost feel jealous," she adds in a whisper. "Why wasn't she able to be *that* patient and indulgent with me?"

"Maybe this is your mother's way of making up for what she did not give you back then?"

"Maybe ..." she responds, as a playful piano tune makes it through the locked door.

We both grow silent, listening to its cheerful, dancing melody. In an uncanny repetition of the past, Elena is overhearing her mother's teaching piano through a locked door, but this time she is not alone and, in a more striking contrast to the past, her mother isn't with some stranger, she is actually taking care of her own granddaughter.

"You can definitely do with some babysitting, even online."

"I can," she exhales. "We actually managed to escape for a walk with Luis the other day ... just the two of us. We made love ... for the first time in months. And I wasn't even drunk," Elena blushes at her confession.

**

As we keep on meeting weekly, spring turns magically into summer. New York is painfully recovering its spaces, its long-lost energy, but music does not return to the Philharmonic, which soon announces the cancellation of the upcoming season. I watch Elena's growing frustration; she is unsettled and often depressed.

Through this time Elena is slowly learning to rely on Luis who is doing his best, helping her to organise online gigs with her fellow musicians and attending the Bandwagon sessions that the orchestra performs across the wounded city.

"He is actually really good at these things," she notices in another discovery.

Her mother keeps showing up for the online piano lessons with her granddaughter with surprising regularity. These sessions soon become part of their routine. Sonia enjoys the hours spent playing and listening to stories about famous musicians. Her progress in piano, but also in Russian, is impressive. Elena is bewildered; her mother has turned into an attentive and patient teacher for her granddaughter.

"She keeps praising Sonia for every small improvement. I cannot believe it!" she says with childish envy.

"In her own way, she is trying to do better," I say, thinking about how my own mother drew princesses over Skype endlessly with my daughter when she was Sonia's age.

**

"You know … I don't feel angry with her anymore," Elena confesses in one of our last sessions. "She didn't have it easy, bringing me up alone in the middle of post-Soviet madness."

Her new-found compassion for her mother helps her accept her own imperfections, and she is slowly becoming a more attentive parent for Sonia. Her bouts of motherly guilt still haunt her from time to time, but she is more able to recognise her limitations without sinking into dramatic conclusions.

As Sonia develops a special bond with her grandmother, Elena regains her own world, freed from her mother's constant judgement and unattainable expectations.

The little American girl and her distant Russian grandmother seem to enjoy their own enchanted musical world. Sonia loves the upright piano she finally gets and spends hours playing with her cat.

***

"The other day my mother told me that she is ready to give up her music school job, to fully focus on her online teaching," Elena announces in one of our final sessions.

"Do you think this may bring her closer?"

"It may … I have the impression that she is considering coming to the States more often."

"How would you feel about it?" I wonder, picking up on her anxiety.

"Hmmm … Why not … We shall see …"

IX

Claire

Paris, France

For our initial session, Claire comes in person to my therapy room in Paris. We are both still blissfully unaware of the pandemic, a faraway storm, still vague and unthreatening.

My doorbell rings perfectly on time and I welcome Claire. In her late forties, she is petite, tense and tight as a spring. After a surprisingly firm handshake, she picks without hesitation one of the two identical leather armchairs – the one near to the door, in case a quick escape is necessary – and looks around my office extensively and inquisitively.

"You mentioned an introductory chat on your website, so here I am, trying to see how therapy with you may help," Claire warns me before I can ask any uncomfortable questions. Her velvety dark eyes put me on trial.

"What can I help you with?" I reply, in an attempt to redirect her attention from my persona to her own agenda.

"I am not entirely sure yet," she admits.

The first thing about Claire that I notice is how well composed and perfectly together she seems. The earthy palette of her carefully chosen clothes highlights the glow of her light brown skin.

"My office is just around the corner," Claire comments, pleased about this lucky coincidence, letting me know that fitting therapy into her busy schedule represents a considerable effort. She has recently been transferred to Paris by a large American corporation – another upward professional move for her.

"A very exciting position, I must say," she adds, pleased with herself.

Impenetrable and sleek, Claire reports on her professional achievements, and once again I hit the protective wall she is building.

"Congratulations on the promotion and your career, but could you tell me what brings you here today?" I try my usual opening question, fighting a wave of boredom mounting inside. Fighting with sleepiness as Claire reports on her daily business in the months to come is not really an option I envisage.

"It's just a question of maintenance," she explains indulgently. "You know how Americans do it? They are all in therapy."

"But you are not American, are you?" I hope to exploit the breach that her very British pronunciation offers me.

"No, not really," she responds, and her perfectly aligned white teeth shine as she smiles.

She fills me in efficiently with the intricate story of her childhood, packed in a well-organised pitch: daughter of a British diplomat and an Indian woman – Bengali to be precise – her early childhood was spent in India. When she turned ten and her younger brother five, their parents moved to England. Her two parents are now dead. Her younger brother is her only family now; he lives near London with his wife and three kids.

Her past is complex and fascinating. Her current Parisian life seems dull. Claire does not engage in any activities outside of work; her social circle is reduced to a few colleagues, in whom she expresses no interest, and a French teacher she openly dislikes.

"Why now? Is there anything in your present life that is troubling you?" I try to break in again.

"I am not completely sure …," she shrugs with a surprisingly timid smile. "There is something about being here that I find uncomfortable."

"Uncomfortable? Could you tell me more?"

"I always thought I would love living in Paris. Who wouldn't? But … it has not been pleasant at all. And I do not seem to be able to learn French," she admits, her eyes drifting towards the Parisian rooftops visible from the window. Claire is puzzled by this unexpected blockage. "I am fluent in Spanish and reasonably good in Bengali. I always considered myself a quick learner, reaching my goals through hard work, but this time … I don't seem to be getting a grip on the French language, it just doesn't stick. I am so annoyed with myself," she acknowledges. My own boredom has dissipated; at last I have something to work on, with this sentiment clearly expressed. Her linguistic struggle may reveal some bigger truths.

We agree to meet weekly and, as Claire leaves, a thin fragrance suggests some exuberant faraway places to me. I remain with a vague sense of bafflement and annoyance. Despite Claire's apparent directness, she has not revealed much about her real agenda.

What is she is really looking for?

***

Later that evening, as I stand in my kitchen preparing a pissaladière onion and anchovy tart, tears streaming from my eyes as I peel and cut the onions, I reflect on my first session with Claire. With her many layers of pale cashmere, her persona appears to my imagination as an onion waiting to be peeled.

***

My doubts about Claire's readiness to commit to therapy are confirmed when she cancels our next session.

"Sorry, work has been crazy," she emails me, asking to postpone.

Then she cancels again and keeps rescheduling for a few weeks, until the pandemic unravels across the European continent, and all my sessions have to be moved to online video calls.

As I rediscover her face on my screen, composed and impeccably made up again – no surprises there – I am startled by her surroundings – a plain white wall, an empty bookshelf, and a basic Ikea lamp in the corner of her room, as in a cheap hotel room or furnished apartment. This bare interior contradicts with the sleek façade Claire displays. I wonder whether she is connecting from someone else's place, but she quickly dissipates any doubts about the flat being her own.

"This is only temporary, why spend money on it? And the location is convenient, only five minutes' walk from the office," she explains with no trace of regret or embarrassment.

"How long are you planning to stay in Paris?" I ask.

"Maybe another year or two. Anyway, I prefer to keep my belongings to the minimum. It makes the next move easier," she adds, watching my face closely.

"How many times have you moved in your life?"

"Oh … I have not kept count. Large corporations such as mine move what they call 'high-potentials' around every two to three years in different jobs and countries. One just gets used to it."

Keeping her luggage light seems to preclude human attachments as well – in her early forties Claire has no romantic partner, no children, no pets.

"My parents always said that I was quick to adapt – a real chameleon, they used to say. I picked up the local dialect wherever we went on holiday, I made friends …"

Looking at her minimalist room I realise that this time she has made sure there is not much to adapt to. Her resistance towards French may also be an unconscious act of rebellion. Is the chameleon simply tired of its perpetual metamorphosis?

"This constant adaptation sounds exhausting, doesn't it?" I ask.

"Exhausting? It's actually been fine ... but sometimes I start losing track of things," she offers tentatively.

"What do you mean by 'losing track of things'?"

"You know ... memories," she replies, and this time I can see for a second some fear mounting to the shiny surface of her eyes. We are walking on the thin ice of her mistrust.

"Any particular incidents that you have forgotten?"

"If I have forgotten them, how would I know?" she drops, her voice vacillating between fear and anger.

"Sure ... When did you realise that you have started to forget things?"

"A few months ago ... when ..." she stops halfway through her sentence, her lips closing in a straight tight line.

"Is it when you first contacted me?"

She nods, and I exhale, the motive of her first visit finally clarified. Claire keeps silent for a moment and I wait for her to be ready to finally elaborate on her reason for seeing me.

"A few days before I contacted you I had spoken with my brother ... We rarely do these days, he is too busy with his kids. I complained about not being able to pick up French, and he said something that has been rattling me since then."

"What did he say?"

"That it reminded him how I had lost my French after my summer stay in France ... and my stubborn refusal to speak French after that trip had saved him from being sent away later on. The thing is, I have no recollection at all from that trip."

"Did you find out more about that trip, for example, when he thinks it took place?"

"I tried to make him me tell more, but I was afraid he would think I was going crazy … It seems it was over our first summer holidays back home. Funny how he thinks of England as 'home'; for me it was just another foreign place, different from everything I knew at that point."

"It is not unusual for siblings to have an entirely different experience of the same events. But at least you can pick his brains to reconstruct some of what was going on at the time. So you must have been around ten at the time, right?"

"I guess so. I should remember things happening at that age, shouldn't I?"

"Did your brother give you any other details about that trip?"

"No, not really, he was only five back then. Am I going crazy?"

"I wouldn't say so … but a memory loss can be scary. It is not unusual though. We can forget things for a variety of reasons," I try to reassure her. "At that time you may have been shaken by your recent relocation to Europe; you had just lost the familiar environment that was making you feel safe and at home, such as some friends or a house."

Claire listens to me listing her childhood losses with a blank face, not letting any emotion out, but across the screen, I can sense the tension emanating from her.

"Why would your parents want to send you off to France at that stressful time?"

"My mother was absolutely in love with anything French. I remember us going to Paris for a weekend right after our move."

"So, you remember *that* trip?"

"Yes, I do. I always had an excellent memory. I don't remember many details, but still … my mother was very excited. We climbed the Eiffel Tower and did a lot of shopping. She always wanted us to speak French. We had to practise ordering food in the restaurants. For her, it was an ultimate sign of social ascendance."

"What kind of relationship did you have with your mother?"

"Distant. She was mostly interested in her social life, constantly going out to play tennis or bridge. We were often left in the care of nannies or babysitters."

The bitter note in Claire's voice creates a crack in her neat façade. Her cheeks turn red with anger.

"Could there be a link between your mother's passion for France and your resistance to learning French?"

She stares at me silently, then finally nods. "There may be one … I never thought of it that way," she admits. "Will I be able to recall that trip?"

Goal oriented, Claire is unwilling to lose precious time on any unnecessary delving that would typically be part of any therapeutic journey.

"You may start remembering some of it as we move forward … But why is it so important for you to remember that trip?"

"I don't really know … I find it terrifying not having a clue about something that happened to me," she responds with clear anxiety.

So we make a deal, our goals have broadened from trying to understand her resistance to learning French to recovering some lost childhood memories. I secretly hope to see even more substantial scope emerge as we move forward.

***

The morning before our third session, when Claire opened her fridge for a pack of cream cheese for her breakfast, something significant happened, leading to the first turning point in her therapy. As she was reaching for the cheese between the packs of yogurt, a French pop song from the '80s playing on the radio popped into her consciousness. She dropped the cheese on the floor, a wave of uneasiness hitting her immediately.

"I just felt like I was going to be sick. This had never happened before … I couldn't touch the cheese anymore, and had to switch off the radio. What was it?" she whispers.

"Is it a song you knew?"

"Not that I can remember," Claire replies, not convinced by her own words. "I found it later on Spotify but could not listen to it … It's a very sad song actually," she adds staring at me quizzically.

"You said that you recognised it as a song from the '80s?"

"This is what they said on the radio, it was a whole programme about French pop in the '80s."

"Isn't that when you were supposedly spending a summer in France?"

She nods, looking shaken.

"Would you like us to listen to this song together?" I decide to take a chance at helping her with this anxiety-producing task.

"Ok." After some hesitation she sighs and searches on her computer.

Then Francis Cabrel's voice reaches us at the same time, recognisable by his accent from the south-west of France, his melodies and his guitar playing. *'Je l'aime à mourir'* – I love her to death – a song that even today most French people know off by heart. We both freeze, in a shared effort to detect something that led to that morning's incident. Claire is letting the song in, her eyes riveted to the screen, but I doubt she is seeing my face on it; crumbs of her past finally resurfacing.

"I do remember something …" she whispers her eyes wide

open. "We sat in bed and ate that cream cheese with our fingers." She stops abruptly, her eyes riveted to the screen but seeing something else.

"Please, do not stop, keep going ..." I murmur, hardly breathing.

"A girl ... a friend of mine. We were taking turns at stealing the cheese from the fridge, then ate it with our fingers in bed."

"Did you speak French together?"

"I guess we did ..."

This is how far Claire goes this time. During her stay in France back in the '80s, Cabrel's songs topped the charts and were played everywhere. She was ten and had a friend for company.

"I loved that girl, I am sure ..."

"Can you remember her name?"

"No, I cannot ...," she admits, tears of frustration in her eyes.

We stay there, listening to the final notes of the song, with the guitar arpeggios fading out melancholically.

"Will I remember more?" she wonders.

"You probably will ... but let's take all the time you need to recover those memories," I say, sensing a vague fear deep down inside.

Claire has buried these events securely out of reach, possibly to protect the little girl in her who could not deal with the feelings associated with those memories. Should she remember? Or is she better off with that small part of her life forgotten? Once these memories are set free, they may trigger an avalanche of consequences. I choose to ignore these thoughts as Claire keeps staring at me silently, waiting for the next step in our quest.

"Maybe I should call my brother again," she suddenly recovers her composed adult self.

She is ready to act but the prospect of another conversation about the past with her brother is making her twitch.

"We rarely talk … and certainly never about the past," she confirms as I ask how she feels about that idea.

"Why is that?"

"I always felt that we were completely different … He always had it easier." Her old grudge gives her beautiful face a childish and sulky expression.

"In what way?"

"When we moved, he was too young to remember much of our life back in India. I resented him for not being homesick, not missing anything from our previous life. And he was allowed to stay home. For some reason our parents decided not to send him to boarding school, which was unusual in their circles."

"Why do you think?"

"I never knew … They just said they preferred him to stay with them, after all the moving around we had had."

"But this is inconsistent with sending you off to France for a whole summer just after the move to England," I say, feeling a sharp burst of anger about this apparent unfairness. "You went to boarding school, didn't you?"

"I did … I told you – I had it much worse …" she whispers in a little girl's voice.

"This sounds pretty unfair," I translate her young feelings into some adult words.

"I guess it does," Claire echoes me. "Do you think I should talk about it with him again?"

I gladly agree with her plan. By breaking the long-established family rules of keeping silent about the past, Claire has a chance to fill in the voids of her lost memories. I also secretly hope she may mend her relationship with her only sibling. Claire, with her tendency to keep her luggage light, is obviously lonely. The slightly ironic, condescending tone that she usually uses when referring to her brother and 'his three kids' covers a sore spot. Does she feel excluded from his family? Is it another 'unfairness' that she keeps re-enacting by refusing to get closer? Can she secretly be envious of his family life?

***

"Camille!" she blurts as if she had been waiting for our next session to finally let out the French girl's name. "James actually remembered it very well; it seems I kept talking about her after I returned from France."

This is the first time I see Claire so excited.

In addition, James insisted that after that trip she had 'some crazy ideas about adopting that French girl'. At the time he actually took it badly, as it meant his sister preferred her to him as a sibling.

"This is the first time you have mentioned your brother's name." Before rushing for the resolution of the mystery, I am determined to capitalise on this newly opened channel between the siblings.

"OK, so what?" She is surprised by my change of focus.

"The story of your lost memories is also that of your childhood, which you shared with one person, your brother." She wants to interrupt me, but I keep going. "To recover these memories may also be an opportunity for recovering the relationship with your only sibling."

Claire gets sulky and then even angry. "I am not sure there is anything to recover," she drops. "He never showed any interest in my whereabouts ... The guy is completely absorbed with his wife and kids, playing the perfect family man," she adds bitterly.

"You sound upset as you say this," I notice.

"I am not upset any more. I don't care," she insists, but her dark eyes are wet.

"Not upset anymore? Were you upset when you were younger?"

"Of course I was! James was my parents' favourite. He always knew what to do to please them," she concludes peevishly.

"Anybody else in your past who was 'playing a perfect family man' and showed no interest in you?"

"My father …?" she responds hesitantly.

"Was he? Tell me a little more about him."

"He kept boasting about being a good family man, a great father, but I always knew that he was not interested in me in the slightest. It was all pretence! At the first opportunity, I was sent away."

"And do you still resent your brother for this unjust treatment …?"

She neither protests nor confirms.

"And what about your mother in all this?"

"My father often repeated that I was my mother's girl … but she would usually object jokingly that I couldn't really speak Bengali properly."

"Jokingly? What a cruel way of joking!"

"I never thought about her as cruel … but you are probably right. She was often cruel to me."

"Does James speak Bengali?"

"No, he wasn't expected to have learnt it; he was young when we left India."

"Another injustice," I comment, and she nods promptly.

Each time she mentions her mother, the question of language comes up. During their time in India, Claire was sent to a British school, and Bengali was strictly reserved for her exchanges with her mother and the members of her side of the family. At that time she felt closer to her, spent a lot of time playing near her when her mother received visits from her numerous cousins and aunts from Kolkata.

"I still remember their joyous chatter in Bengali, their laughter and the aromas of the meals they would share during my father's absence," she says dreamily. "All that was lost when we moved to England."

With the move, came new rules. Claire was accepted at once by a prestigious boarding school where she had to work hard to catch up with the other girls. Her mother was around less often, busy rebuilding her social life in a new place. With the move, Claire unburdened herself from the past, her Indian ties and her language. Bengali was soon downscaled to a few weekly exchanges over the phone with her maternal grandparents or aunts, and a polite 'how do you do' for her mother's Indian friends' rare visits.

Growing up, Claire sensed that her poor mastery of her mother's language divided them, but could not really do much about it. At home they only spoke English, and the growing pressure at school and her parents' expectations for her academic performance were building up, not allowing much space for anything unessential.

"I simply gave up at some point," she recognises. "My mother always assumed I would just speak Bengali; she never helped me with it. Soon after the move she stopped talking to me in her native tongue … then stopped talking altogether," she concludes bitterly.

"I remember when you mentioned your French teacher, you said something about her having 'unreasonable expectations'. This sounds strangely similar to your mother's attitude towards your learning Bengali," I bring her back to her current struggles.

"She does have ridiculous expectations and always makes this typical French face, you know," she mimics a disappointed grimace. "My mother never did that but any time I would make a mistake or use the wrong word in Bengali, she would just glare at me silently, surprised by my dumbness … So I guess there is some parallel there …"

"You clearly dislike your French teacher. Have you thought about changing to a different one? Somebody more supportive, who wouldn't wince at your mistakes?"

She looks at me, slightly bewildered by this option.

"You could not change your mother, but you can change your French teacher, can't you?"

"I guess I could …"

"What about joining a language school when the lockdown is over? More social interactions in Paris wouldn't hurt, would they?"

"Hmmm …" she shrugs dismissively. "It will be full of foreigners conversing in their bad French, with all kinds of terrible accents …," she says, making the same disgusted face her mother used to make at her childhood mistakes in Bengali.

When I point out the similarity to Claire, she instantly shuts up – a polished seashell, left on the sand by the unfriendly tide.

***

In the days before our next session, Claire was scrolling through her social media, looking at the grim posts from her distant acquaintances locked down all around the globe. She found herself typing 'Camille' into the search field … and a surname popped up promptly into her mind 'Fleur' – this was the French girl's flowered name.

"I now remember my parents joking about that funny name, my father kept calling her 'Poppy' … She had this wonderful red hair, pretty unusual for French girls, from what I can remember."

As Claire typed 'Camille Fleur' into the search bar, several female faces appeared on her screen, but only one was framed with unmistakably fiery curls.

"I would never recognise her if I met her in the street, but the name and the hair … I was sure it was her, Camille."

"Did you reach out to her?" I ask, already knowing the answer.

"No, I couldn't," she admits. "Her profile is private, I could not find out anything about her life. But it looks like she still lives in Paris."

"From what you remembered so far, it seems that you cared a lot about Camille Fleur and then she vanished from your life, probably like many other friends that you had to leave behind when your family moved to England," I say to Claire, who looks out of the window, her face turned into a desolate mask.

"I feel so guilty," she whispers.

"Guilty? What about?"

"About letting her down."

"But you were only ten back then and she lived on the opposite side of the Channel. This was before the internet and video calls, I guess. Only your respective parents had the capacity to help you continue your friendship, but for some reason they didn't."

"I wasn't a good friend to her," she stubbornly insists.

I imagine that Claire has her reasons to feel that she let the French girl down, but she has no memories that would explain these feelings. She is desperate to recall the events of that summer to challenge her belief that she cannot be a reliable friend.

"Did you make other close friendships, after Camille vanished from your life?"

"No, I didn't," she responds bluntly, too much pain hidden behind her dry eyes.

After that French holiday Claire made sure she did not let anybody else down by avoiding relationship commitments of any kind.

"Do you think this has something to do with the guilt you felt about letting your only best friend down?"

"That sounds crazy, doesn't it?" she acquiesces with despair.

"No matter how crazy this may sound, the loss of Camille has impacted you in many ways, one of them being your reluctance to develop intimate relationships," I respond, recalling my first impressions of her – that unpleasant experience of being presented with a solid wall instead of an entrance.

Her distrust is based on misplaced memories; without access to the events of that summer trip we can hardly confirm or challenge this damaging belief.

"What about romantic relationships?" I ask the burning question about the area of her life that Claire has carefully avoided since the beginning of her therapy.

"I am too embarrassed to answer …," she recognises but, after a long pause, she continues: "I never let anything like that happen."

A few times, some insistent man made it to a second date, but Claire always found a way to backpedal.

"When anybody gets too close, I panic and make sure they disappear from my surroundings entirely," she recognises, almost proud of the efficiency of her defences.

"When we first met I felt that you kept me at arm's length, but now things are starting to change …" I try my best shot. "Are you starting to let some closeness develop here?"

"It is only because you are my therapist. I am paying you for this and can actually let you down without this affecting you in any major way," she drops as dismissively as she can and smiles sarcastically at her screen.

She is certainly right. Claire could vanish, I would feel sad and disappointed, but this would not affect my personal life directly. The limited nature of our relationship helps her make a timid step in the risky direction towards others. Will she ever be able to extend this newly acquired experience to other more significant relationships?

Claire

Somehow I feel that Camille could help, if Claire could overcome her shame and reach out to her childhood friend.

```
I always suspected you would reappear one day

        I am sorry I didn't try to contact you before

Please, don't be. A few years ago I was not ready to
talk about this. Things were bumpy for a while

        Bumpy?

I drank, but I am sober now

        Are you married?

No, I am not. Are you?

        No

Shame WhatsApp didn't exist at the time … we would not
have lost touch with each other
```

Claire sends me a screen shot of this first WhatsApp chat with Camille a few minutes before our session. When we connect, she is still visibly shaken by what followed that brief initial exchange.

"We have spoken over the phone several times since then. I ended up telling her about my memory loss."

For some reason Camille was not surprised that Claire did not recall the events of that summer. She did not volunteer any clues either, which made Claire only more anxious to fill the gaps.

"We spoke in French … it's strange. It all came back at once … Camille's voice hasn't changed. Also, she remembered clearly the Cabrel song and the cream cheese."

At the end of their conversation, Camille asked, "Did you really forget everything?" Then she added, "I envy you; I would give anything to stop remembering …"

Her words have stayed with Claire and, as we speak, they keep resonating in her mind.

"She offered to go for a walk, but I am not sure I want to keep digging ..."

Claire stares at me, as if I could restore her obliviousness and free her of this dilemma. I sense her anxiety and fear, but we both know that there is no way back; we have activated forces that cannot be stopped. Camille has a story to tell, one that has tied them together.

"I asked her for their old address," she resumes her tale. "The house was sold long ago ... I drove there this morning. It was outside of the permitted one-kilometre-from-home, but I had to see that house again."

Driving through the deserted city, Claire felt dizzy with excitement and anxiety. She hoped that going back to the place where she had met Camille would bring her memories back, without having to deal with Camille's emotions, in addition to her own.

"I didn't want to get too emotional in front of Camille," she acknowledges.

"What would happen then?" I enquire, as Claire keeps her upper lip stiff and her eyes dry.

"She might find me ridiculous ..."

"Ridiculous?" I am used to witnessing clients' discomfort at displaying difficult emotions, but Claire stands out with her avoidance of displaying vulnerability in front of anybody, me included.

"Camille, your childhood friend, may find you ridiculous? Are you sure you are not talking about somebody else?"

"What do you mean?" she responds, the usual wariness returning to her voice.

"I am just wondering if this fear of being ridiculed when showing your feelings may come from further away."

"Well ... With my mother I always knew I shouldn't cry. She

would get annoyed if I ever did. Once she scolded me when I cried about not wanting to return to boarding school after a long weekend at home: 'British girls know how to control themselves, didn't they teach you that at your school?'" Claire looks away and towards the invisible window; her eyes lost in the greyness that has now taken hold of the Parisian skies.

"Do you think your mother was happy in London?"

"Clearly, she wasn't. She became bitter. She felt she didn't fit in with my father's circle of top civil servants. Many of them had exotic wives, who mainly kept to themselves. But why take it out on me?" Claire wonders sourly.

"Parents often project their own unhappiness onto their children … Which isn't fair in any way. And now it looks like you are carrying a burden that you have inherited unknowingly."

"I do feel resentful, you are right," she acknowledges, a sudden wariness invading the velvet of her eyes, which echoes the dark clouds invading the skies outside my window.

An intense sadness fills the space between us.

Claire's mother resented her daughter's Britishness, but she actively pushed it onto her by sending her to a boarding school and no longer speaking Bengali with her. With the summer trip to France, she unconsciously made Claire experience the same emotional struggle that she was dealing with in London – in that French household, her daughter felt foreign and alienated. As I look at the adult Claire, her protective layers stuck to her core, I feel for her deeply.

"Anyway, when I finally reached the suburban street near Paris where the house should have been, a hideous block of flats was standing there instead."

The whole area, emptied by the lockdown, was ghostly and surreal, similar to her fragmented memories of that distant

French summer. The café on the opposite corner hadn't changed though. She remembered men sitting at the terrace, a few shabby tables on the street, drinking and speaking loudly. They used to scare Camille and her as they walked back from school – "Don't look, keep talking to me, keep walking," Camille would whisper, squeezing her hand tight. Now, through the dirty windows, Claire saw chairs stacked upside down on the tables. The place looked abandoned, with a few dried-up plants in one corner.

Claire sat in her car, just in front of what used to be the entrance of Camille's old house, reluctant to leave the safety of her vehicle. She felt her memories moving slowly under the surface of her mind, ready to burst out. But she didn't feel ready, not just yet.

"I remembered Camille's room. In the evenings, when she was doing her homework, I would look out of the window, feeling homesick. The plain yellowish wall was still there. It used to block the view from Camille's bedroom. I couldn't call my parents, international calls were too expensive."

Her parents didn't call much either. Claire remembered talking with them a couple of times only, and those were awkward conversations, as Camille's parents would not leave her in the room alone.

As Claire shares these bits of freshly recovered memories, I watch her face slowly swept by a complex dance of emotions – longing, fear and sadness come to the surface like bubbles on water. She finally lets her tears out and cries silently without hiding. Letting her tears fall, Claire watches my face on her screen, seeking confirmation that I do not find her ridiculous. What she does not know is how easily I connect with the little Claire, who is trapped far from home, lonely and confused. I also came to France as a teenager, on a school trip. The family I was staying with was not particularly warm, caring or interested in making me feel welcome.

Nobody wondered whether I was hungry or comfortable. I felt unwanted, superfluous. Why had they signed up for this, apart from the allowance money they received? I wonder to this day.

**

That evening I finally go out for a run, trailing my residual sadness behind me. On the bridge above the Seine a police patrol checks the occasional passers-by for their documentation confirming their reasons for being outside during lockdown.

"You should not run outside of your arrondissement," a police officer reproaches me sternly, his steel eyes fixed on my uncovered face (running without a mask is allowed).

"But I am only seven hundred meters away from where I live," I try to protest.

"It doesn't matter, madam, the rules are the rules." No trace of a smile on his masked face.

I end up avoiding a fine and stroll back to the safety of my flat with a residual feeling of uneasiness.

At the dinner table I laugh the incident off with my husband, but somewhere deep down in my belly there is fear. Being questioned in this way by an unfriendly policeman sends me instantly back to my post-Soviet past. Back then I was all-too familiar with the feeling of being in an unfriendly environment, having to watch every step, expecting any kind of catastrophe to happen any moment. I had never expected though to be caught up by this kind of fear on the Pont Mirabeau.

**

A few weeks later the lockdown has eased and at least some of our freedoms are restored. We all suspect that this return to normality is only temporary; the outside air is filled with tension. For Claire, the lifting of restrictions comes with a new dilemma.

"Camille suggested meeting up again and going for a walk, and I am terrified at the prospect," she texts me in an unusual break from her own stiff boundaries. "And I said yes."

When Claire finally returns to my screen, something is subtly different about her. I cannot identify what exactly has changed, but the energy she emanates is lighter.

"I saw Camille …" With her first words comes the possible explanation.

They met at the Palais Royal and walked around in circles, or rather in parallelograms, following the implacable logic of the garden's classical space. The benches were all too wet to sit down on, but the café under the arcades was miraculously open for take-away. They sipped their coffees as they stood under the bare trees, checking the heavy sky for an inevitable shower.

Claire did not know what to say, where to start. She avoided meeting her friend's uncovered face and her bright eyes. Camille sensed her unease and did all the talking, which came to her easily as if they were old friends re-united after a short separation.

"After you had left, I dreamed for years about coming to see you in London …" Camille says, making Claire shrivel up with shame.

"I hoped you would come, but my parents told me that it wasn't possible anymore. I never quite knew why but suspected you were upset with me."

"Upset with you?" Camille seemed genuinely bewildered as she stopped and stared at her friend with her green eyes, whose unusual colour Claire now remembered with resolute clarity.

As they stood there, in the middle of a deserted arcade, the wind blowing dead leaves, making them swirl all around them, something clicked in Claire's mind. She felt sick with disgust, fear and inexplicable guilty excitement.

"I was relieved we had our masks on again," she recognises. "I could not bear seeing her face at that point ..."

"Why? What were you afraid of seeing?"

"I don't know ... Some terrible traces that her trauma had left."

They didn't move for a while, Claire was grateful to Camille who kept silent, letting the lost memories come back slowly, in big, dark swells.

"I am so sorry ..." Claire finally whispered, as the image slowly came back to her of them lying in bed, as close to each other as possible, trying to make no noise, hoping that Camille's stepfather would forget about them. He never did. Claire could now remember his heavy frame passing the door of the bedroom, then closing it quietly behind. He would always get angry at finding Claire in her friend's bed. He would order her to return to her own bed, close her eyes tight and go to asleep. She would be terrified and obey, even though leaving her friend alone in her bed made her sick to the stomach.

"Go, and please do as he says," Camille would whisper in her ear, pushing her gently out from under the duvet.

Then he would take her place. She still remembered the bed's creaking under his thick-set body.

"I would lie there, in the darkness, trying to lose my senses, not hear his heavy breathing ..."

This happened each evening during Claire's stay. She tried to convince her friend to talk to her mother about these nocturnal visits, but Camille was adamant she had to protect her mother who 'suffered from ill health' and needed her husband to 'take care of them both'.

"Telling her this would kill my mother," she then said to Claire.

This was exactly what the monster would tell his stepdaughter every night before finally leaving her alone. She believed him, as her mother was often unwell, unable to leave her room for days in a row.

Witnessing the abuse had left Claire feeling dirty and, despite Camille's reassurance, guilty for keeping silent, as if failing to protect her friend had made her an accomplice.

"When did it stop?" Claire asked finally, when the heavy knot in her throat eased slightly.

"A couple of years later … and only because I hit puberty."

"Did you ever tell your mother?"

"No, she never knew. They separated several years later … but I was living in downtown Paris by then."

When Claire finally returned home, her parents did not ask many questions, or maybe Claire kept avoiding answering them until they stopped. Her mother was disappointed about her lack of progress in French, which she simply refused to speak. Claire never talked about Camille's secret and soon her mind suppressed the episode altogether.

Claire reports Camille's final words, perplexed: "You probably saved my sanity back then … I was not alone with this anymore, even after you left, you remained my best friend."

Camille recalled in minute detail the events of that summer; some of them nevertheless included happier moments, which helped her survive, such as the stories told by Claire in English, the secret language her French stepfather did not understand. The protagonists of these fairy tales were young, rebellious girls, who defied monsters and ran away, crossing the sea for a better life elsewhere.

In her real life, things were different. The monsters were stronger, more powerful, and both girls had to carry the wounds of that childhood abuse for years.

"I replayed those stories in my head for years … and this is maybe why I ended up writing books for children," Camille added, taking a book out of her tote bag. "So, I have you to thank for this as well."

Claire brings up the book in front of her camera – on the cover are two girls in pyjamas running through a field of sunflowers, trying to escape a powerful storm threatening them from above.

"I read it ... and ordered the whole series translated into English for my nieces. I wish I had not lost Camille for all these years," she concludes with regret.

"Will you be meeting again?"

"I don't know," she responds honestly. "So much time has passed ... I am still not sure whether she has forgiven me." Claire retreats to her familiar shame, her eyes wandering to her friend's book.

"Why don't we simply listen to what Camille has to say? For all these years, not having any contact with her, you had to guess, your imagination filling the gaps. As you have read her book now, what does it actually say about the girls?"

"That they are great friends and together they are strong enough to brave any dangers," she responds, like a good student.

"Right. And you are that great friend who inspired these stories. Camille has been clear – in the short time of your visit you made a difference to her life. Wouldn't you agree that this confirms that at least once in your life you were a brilliant friend?"

Claire nods, still unconvinced, but a new hope is bringing light to her melancholy eyes.

***

"Would you like to resume meeting in person again?" I ask Claire when the restrictions are eased and some clients start to visit my office again.

"No, thank you, I'd rather stick to the screen, at least for now."

I am slightly disappointed, but have to respect her preference. Her shame, reactivated by the encounter with Camille, has made her retreat back to her worn-out protective shell.

"My brother called this weekend to thank me for the books."

Not only did James call, but his three daughters were in front of the screen as well, eager to tell their distant aunt how much they loved the two friends' adventures. Claire had not seen them in a while and was surprised to find out how bright and engaged they all seemed. When the girls finally left the adults alone, James initiated the conversation about their past again.

"Are those the books written by *your* Camille?" he asked, even if the answer was no mystery to him. "I have been reading them to the girls at bed time … Are you actually one of the characters?"

"I guess I may well be …" Claire responds, for the first time acknowledging her part in Camille's writing.

"Have you met her again for real?"

James sounded excited; he wanted to learn everything about the French friend whom his lonely sister had searched for and found. Before they hung up, he invited Claire to visit as soon as travel could resume. Maybe he had said that before, but somehow this was the first time Claire did not feel annoyed by the invitation.

"I never felt at ease in his home. They are all just so … perfect," she explains.

"Are you planning to go?" I don't hide my hope.

"I may … I promised them I'd bring a copy signed by the author," she sighs, anxious at the self-made opportunity to meet Camille again.

"Camille will surely be thrilled to know that your nieces loved her books," I comment with a smile.

"Actually you will be happy about something else as well." She steers away from the topic with an introductory sentence that usually warns me about some important behavioural break-through. "I actually signed up for a language school; they are resuming their offline classes next week."

"I am happy indeed to hear that," I confirm.

"You are probably right. I could do with more French-speaking people around me ..."

"Or simply more people?" I make her smile this time.

"You know, reading Camille's books, I've realised that my French isn't that awful," she recognises, a faint smile on her lips.

"Might talking with Camille have helped as well?"

"Not sure, we ended up speaking English."

***

A few hours before our next session, in a surprising reversal of her earlier stance, Claire texts me asking if we could meet in my office.

"Of course, I would be happy to see you in person again," I confirm, curious about this sudden willingness to get closer.

As she steps into the room, the first thing I notice is the change of her dress code. The pastel onion layers are gone, and she is wearing a plain white T-shirt and skinny jeans. Only an expensive leather handbag and her perfectly groomed skin reveal her social and financial status.

Claire looks around – seemingly pleased to see my bookshelves again, notices the new climbing plant in the corner and sits down in the same armchair as on her first visit.

"It's strange to be back here ... I actually enjoyed seeing you on my screen, but this time I thought I might as well come to your office," she explains and adds nonchalantly: "The language school isn't far, I could walk from there."

"How has it been?" I do not hide my excitement at the news.

"It's actually quite fun … even if my fellow foreign students' accents are dreadful, as anticipated," she states with an indulgent smile, which has now replaced the original disappointed grimace taken from her mother's emotional palette.

"What about your French teacher then?" I ask.

"I fired her, she was unsupportive and too old-school for my taste," she reports, timidly proud of her progress.

The devastating shame that Claire used to feel at her childhood missteps in Bengali has receded, especially as she witnessed the embarrassment of her fellow students. She still felt awkward and 'too old to expose herself in such a way', but she didn't run away when one of the students, an American woman, suggested having a drink together.

"I don't expect we will be friends or anything, but … it's nice to have somebody to have a drink with after the class, and enjoy the terrace of the nearby café," she concludes.

As she keeps chatting nonchalantly about her French classes, my attention is drifting away – is Claire not telling me something? She waits till the end of the session to tell me the news: "Camille has invited me to her new book signing at a bookshop."

***

This time, as Claire enters, I sense the tense energy she brings with her. As she settles into her armchair, this tension fills the room.

"I will probably not stay in France for much longer," she finally utters.

I realise my disappointment. Deep down I wanted Claire to make peace, not only with French language, but also with the Paris that has been my home for the past twenty years.

"I know I don't belong here …," she says sadly, then she adds, "nor anywhere else for that matter, but it is not here that I want to try."

She finally meets my eyes, letting me see her confusion.

"What has prompted your decision?" I wonder.

"Camille and I had a very long conversation …"

They met on a terrace to celebrate the reopening of the cafés. For the very first time they sat in front of each other, in a disorientating physical closeness after all the social distancing. With just a round coffee table between them, Claire was reminded of the time when they had shared Camille's bed, the place of her torture, but also where her first stories were born in a rebellious act of resistance.

"You know, as I looked at her in the middle of this café, I realised how comfortably settled she is here."

They discussed Paris, this city that Camille loves, with its riverbanks, its cafés. Camille naturally switched to French … "This place is my family, my home, my everything really." Her words struck Claire, painfully highlighting her own feeling of homelessness.

"When I returned to my flat, I was devastated," Claire shares with sadness. "I just felt so foreign compared to her," she looks away again.

"Foreign? How does that feel to you?"

Slightly annoyed, Claire stumbles at my question. "I don't know … You should know yourself what I mean, shouldn't you?" she fires back defensively.

She is right of course.

"Yes, I do know how 'foreign' feels *to me*, but I would like to understand how it feels *to you*."

The feeling is as familiar as it is unsettling to her. She selects her words.

"Different. Voiceless. Unwanted … Lonely?" She finally meets my eyes and lets me see her pain.

"Lonely …," I echo.

"I never thought I was lonely," she admits.

"Until you met up with Camille again?" I wonder, and she nods.

For Claire, Camille's natural love for her city, or the apparent effortlessness with which she puts her experiences into words and images, only highlights her own inability to speak French, her subtle but constant feeling of not fitting in.

"When did you first feel this 'foreign'?"

"For sure when we moved to London. Everything felt alien, but I quickly figured out that it wasn't the 'everything', but me … I was foreign. Nobody, not even my brother, could understand how much I missed our old life in Delhi – the house, the maid, my old school, my friends … "

"What about your mother? Did she understand?"

"No, she wasn't interested, too busy with her own activities; running to the social gatherings she hated, playing tennis with friends she disliked …"

"Probably desperately trying to escape her own feeling of foreignness?" I offer her.

She smiles bitterly, but accepts my guess.

"So your parents left you alone with your mourning … The little Claire was lonely and the only dear friend she made during those times was abused in front of her and taken away from her abruptly," I summarise the story of her childhood. We sit in silence for a minute, and I have to resist offering her a hug. I pass her a tissue, and this is probably as much tenderness as she can accept at this stage.

"Thank you," she whispers, wiping her mascara-stained eyes.

Claire

She looks like a ten year old for a second.

"I booked my train tickets. It's my oldest niece's tenth birthday next weekend, and James insisted I should come." She quickly recovers her self-contained adult persona. "And I have a book to deliver, after all."

She pulls her handbag towards her, takes the book out and shows me proudly the hand-written note on the cover page: *'To Poppy, from her wonderful aunt's old best friend!'*

"So, you went to Camille's book signing?"

"I did," she confirms looking at the book, entitled 'Crossing the Channel'.

"What's this story about?" I ask, and she passes me the book, still wary of sharing this symbolic artefact of her friendship with Camille, but also of her trauma.

On its cover, two little girls in flowery dresses are standing on a boat deck, holding hands. The red-head must be Camille, and the other girl is taller, with long dark hair.

"This one is you, isn't she?" I say, and she nods. "What's her name?"

"Poppy, just like my oldest niece ... When I told Camille about the coincidence she was thrilled."

"Poppy is a very lucky girl!" I add and hand her the book back, which she does not return to her bag, but leaves lying on the table.

"She is ... She recently got a smartphone and asked James for my number; since then we have been texting each other," she shares with bewilderment.

"You seem surprised?"

"I am. I always thought I just wasn't the kind of person to get along with a kid... I never wanted to have children of my own, or any children around really," she confesses. "I have been avoiding anybody with kids or who could potentially have one ... My

219

brother in the first place," she continues with sincerity.

"You certainly had your reasons for thinking that way before, but it sounds like you are now revaluating some of your earlier decisions. For example, you thought you were not able to be a good friend, until Camille reminded you the contrary," I nod towards the book.

"But it is too late for me to have kids," she remarks, almost with regret.

"But it is certainly not too late to stop avoiding them," I argue.

We both realise that our time is up.

"Let's talk about this again," I offer. "When are you travelling to England?"

"This weekend, and I may stay for a week and work from there ... Can I let you know about next time?"

On the doorstep, as I wish Claire a safe trip, my mind is already racing, imagining all kinds of possible outcomes for her family reunion.

***

"Please could we reschedule?" she writes a few days ahead of our session. "I am extending my stay in the UK for an extra week."

Her email does not mention how her experiment with her brother's family is going. I hope she is enjoying the rapprochement, but I am conscious that it can go wrong. Claire's progress has put her in a vulnerable place. Every time I check my emails, she is on my mind.

In the meantime, the pandemic hardly lets us off the hook. Another wave results in renewed restrictions, the British Isles are closed to international travel again, ease of travel is added to the long list of recent collective losses.

When Claire appears on my screen again, she has been away

from Paris for a few weeks. I am instantly struck by the change of scenery. In contrast to her minimalist Parisian flat, the interior looks as cosy as one can imagine: slightly fading flowery wallpaper, a soft bedhead, a painting of a bucolic cottage on the wall. The English countryside in the garden fills our space with birdsong, children's playful voices, a dog's barking ... Claire, with her formal striped shirt, looks misplaced and confused.

"Now I am completely stuck here and have no idea when I can travel back," she announces. "This is not what I signed up for ..."

"How is it going for you there?"

"It's strange ... Nice in a way, I guess. James is rarely around; he's working at an ongoing building project ... His wife is lovely and I have been helping her with the girls."

It always takes time before we can reach the feeling beneath the surface. Sometimes we have to scratch.

"What a different life from what you are used to ...," I prompt her.

"I am completely lost," she admits. "Just don't know what to make of it. They all behave as if I have always been here ... 'Aunty Claire', what a joke!" she spits out in the most sarcastic tone she can produce.

The evident cosiness of her brother's household is foreign to Claire and, in her usual way she appropriates this foreignness and feels alienated.

"Is it any different from what you expected coming here?"

"It's exactly how I feared it would be," she admits.

"As alienating as you imagined?"

"Worse. I constantly feel like an intruder, a kind of impostor aunty ... But the girls keep taking me for the real one."

"But for them you are the real one," I argue.

Despite her initial discomfort, with the passing weeks I witness

Claire's mood changing. Her stay seems increasingly indefinite, and she does not seem to regret leaving her Paris furnished apartment.

"It's cheap anyway, and I can go back any time really. But what's the point? I am working remotely and not supposed to go to the office for another two months at least ..."

***

We keep our weekly appointments and, with each session, Claire displays small signs of the slow change she is undergoing – a glass pearl bracelet, a handmade gift from Poppy, then a colourful drawing by her youngest niece that I can spot on the wall behind her.

When I acknowledge these little gifts, which illustrate her settling into her brother's family, she smiles timidly. "They can be a little too much for me ... I feel completely foreign at times, especially when they all sit down and play stupid board games ... but they are my only family and, I have to admit, they are quite nice."

James' home is warm and welcoming. Rather than feeling foreign, she is experiencing a new sense of belonging. I want to trust this positive progress as I watch Claire's prolonged family stay. This blissful time goes on for a few weeks, until one day, Claire does not show up for our weekly morning session, for the first time with no warning whatsoever.

As I sit in front of my empty screen, all the doubts I have been keeping at bay fill my mind.

Thirty minutes later, as I am trying to use this extra time to catch up with some emails, Claire's message pops up in the chat box:

"I am so sorry. I overslept. Is it too late to connect?"

This is so unlike her. I agree to postpone my lunch break and we get on a video call. Claire is still wearing pyjamas, her beautiful hair roughly tied back in a loose ponytail.

"I took a day off. My sleep hasn't been great recently," she explains.

She has never mentioned sleeping problems before. Is her turning up late a blunt way of letting me know that something serious is disrupting her sleep?

"What is rattling you?" I enquire, as Claire retreats into silence, unsure whether to trust me with her fears. After a long minute of battling with her thoughts, she finally opts for giving us a chance.

"Every night my nieces insist I give them a goodnight kiss ... and every time I see them in bed I freak out," she tells me, her eyes screaming with pain.

"They are roughly the same age you and Camille were when her step-father was abusing her ..."

"Yes, this keeps coming back to my mind ... This and some other crazy thoughts. I just cannot shake them off."

"You didn't tell me about this before ..."

"No. I didn't want to spoil it. I was scared that if I let these thoughts run free, they would become more real ..."

"Would you like to try? By keeping them inside you may be giving them more power over you."

"Each night when I switch off the light, I start listening to the sounds of the house ... and every cracking of the wooden floor makes my heart race ... I am terrified that my brother might return to my nieces' bedroom ...," Claire whispers, her eyes deadened by fear.

"You suspect your brother of abusing his daughters?"

"In the daytime I don't. Cognitively I know that this is completely unfounded. He is a wonderful father. The girls are happy and I've never seen him doing anything inappropriate, and yet ... these crazy thoughts keep sneaking into my brain."

The intrusive thoughts are haunting Claire every night. The

dark circles around her eyes make more sense now that I realise that she has not been sleeping much. Being around her nieces brings her back to her traumatic summer with Camille's family, over three decades ago.

"Are you extending your stay to be around and keep the girls safe?" I verbalise my guess.

She nods. "Maybe …"

"Have you shared any of this with anybody?"

"Of course not! If my brother knew … he would be shocked and disgusted," she adds with embarrassment.

"Can you think of one person who would understand what you are going through?"

She gazes at me with hope: "Camille? Why, do you think I should tell her?"

"She knows exactly what you went through together. She said that back then you helped her survive by being around. Why not try to let her support you now?"

"But she is the one who was abused. I was just around and didn't do anything to help her," she lets out her darkest truth.

We bump against the same shame again.

"Claire, you were only a child yourself. You did what was within your power – you offered Camille your friendship, which helped her to feel less alienated and alone. With your stories you made her dream, showing her an escape route. Why not let her do the same for you? You could do with the same support right now …"

From her stubborn expression I realise that this is a long shot. When she finally produces an almost invisible nod, I know that at least she will consider it.

"It's probably time for me to go anyway," she concludes. "It has been too long …"

As the travelling restrictions between France and the UK are eased again, Claire books her train ticket to finally return to her supposedly 'normal life', a life that actually does not feel that normal any more. We agree to meet in person again when she returns. On the evening that Claire is travelling back, she keeps coming to my mind.

***

In therapy anything can be turned into an opportunity. In a decade of practising online through video-conferencing, 'anything' has consisted of interruptions on my clients' side of the screen, sudden connection loss, or other minor and major disruptions to the therapeutic conversation.

But now I am facing a totally new kind of disruption, and this time it is happening on my side of the screen. We have finally given in to my daughter's pandemic longing for a dachshund. I have to dog-sit for some parts of the day, the puppy is lying on my lap, quietly for now, he is sweet. Feeling his fast breathing under my hand, I am already anticipating the challenge of several in-person appointments today, starting with Claire.

I write to my clients, warning them in advance about the new pet situation. They all love dogs and it is absolutely fine. Claire is no exception. But how on Earth will I manage?

When she rings the doorbell, I am ready for a storm. The puppy is so excited, as shown by his tail motion. He is curious and wants to be a part of everything. "OK," I think. "Let's trust the process!" and let Claire in.

The initial greetings done, successfully avoiding face licking, we all finally settle – Claire and myself in the armchairs, the puppy on my lap. I try my best to contain him, silently praying for him to calm down. "I could probably drug him to sleep," a fleeting thought crosses my mind as I force myself to give my full attention to Claire, who I haven't seen in person for two months.

"He is cute," she says the obvious thing, then grows silent for a while.

As Claire watches the puppy from a distance, without any sign of wanting to pet him, I observe her. Her dark hair is even longer than usual, making it difficult to see her face properly. I remember her mentioning that she actually enjoyed wearing a mask during the pandemic.

Under her gaze, I slowly realise that I am holding a baby. I think about my daughter holding him in the same way, and how we jokingly comment that she looks like a Renaissance Madonna with Child. Right now, it is me with Claire, with whom we have just started exploring her ambivalent feelings about her nieces and children in general. Talk about unexpected opportunities!

I take a deep breath and, as the puppy starts to doze, I take the plunge: "I guess it looks like I have a new baby."

"It does," she confirms, visibly relieved with my acknowledging the awkwardness of the situation. "I thought I wouldn't mind … but actually I find it disturbing."

"Disturbing?" I had not expected this, there is no way I can get rid of the puppy now – he would cry endlessly if I were to leave him alone.

"Camille has a daughter," she says, her eyes still riveted on the dog.

"You had not mentioned it before." I am taken by surprise.

"No … I am not sure why," she confirms pensively.

"When did she tell you?"

"In our very first chat, and I thought I didn't care … but when we met in that café, she talked about her daughter at length. She is nine now … Camille had her very late." She delivers this in a kind of unemotional tone, steadily avoiding my eyes.

"Do you find Camille's child disturbing?" I verify the only hypothesis that comes to my mind.

"I presumed she had opted out, just like me," she confesses without answering my question directly.

"But she didn't. Have you talked about her choice to have a child late in life?"

"We did. She said that it took her years of therapy to realise that the fact that she was abused as a child does not make her a terrible person or a bad mother," she says and finally meets my eyes.

The puppy on my lap is sleeping tight now, his therapy job done.

"For some reason I can easily imagine Camille as a loving mother …," I continue. "But that brings us back to your choice, I guess."

"I am sorry I didn't start therapy before …," she says with regret – and I can only agree.

"I understand your regret, but I am also glad you are doing this work now."

"I wrote to Camille and we are meeting for a walk. Her daughter will be there. She wants me to meet her."

"How do you feel about it?" I push her to go beyond her regrets.

"I am scared. She might look exactly like Camille at the time … but I want to try to be a good friend," she smiles.

"You have managed to be a good aunt already, and that was challenging," I remind her of the recent relational risks she took.

"You know, these two months at my brother's made me realise that I should probably return to London. Paris isn't really my place. It's just too much work to constantly try to fit in … I need a break," she sighs, looking exhausted.

"Would you also like to be closer to your brother's family?"

"I guess I would. Poppy keeps asking me when I will come back … but I would probably prefer her to visit me in London; we could do things together, I could show her places ... She reminds me of myself, but as a better and luckier version." Claire plays with the glass pearl bracelet that is sparkling on her wrist.

"Luckier, possibly ... Better, we shall see, and you can play a role there," I scale it up for her.

"I guess I could ... They live in the countryside and she is now old enough to enjoy culture ... I would love to take her to a musical or to an exhibition, when all that opens up again ... Camille could come and visit with her daughter ... They are roughly the same age."

Hearing Claire dreaming for the first time about a future that includes somebody else, not just herself and work, fills me with joy.

As I take her to the door, the puppy is still deeply asleep in my arms.

"Can I stroke him?" she asks just before stepping out.

"Of course," I respond, and she tenderly strokes the puppy's velvety fur.

***

That was the last time I saw Claire in my office. She returned to London, where she is renting a slightly cosier flat. She corresponds with Camille, who is planning to finally cross the Channel and visit her with her daughter. Soon after her move Claire decided to switch to a local therapist: "I enjoyed working with you and meeting online was a life-saver, but now I would like to sit in the same room with somebody local."

As Claire feels less alienated, she finally recognises my foreignness. With this thought in mind, I put away my regret of not seeing her anymore, and will remember all the progress she made.

X

Philip

Northumberland, England

With Philip, we are off to a wobbly start. His blurred face is flickering on my screen, only to disappear a few seconds later. I am unsure whether he has heard my greeting at all; I have not even made out his words. He has to move to two different rooms in his cottage before we can hear each other. We both feel worn out from re-starting the call again and again.

"I live in a remote and rural place," Philip explains, somewhat grudgingly.

'Remote' is the word that sticks out. This is exactly how I experience him – his face blurred by the unstable connection and, even with a close-up image, Philip appears distant.

The distance, be it a physical or a cultural one, is obvious. From his initial email I know that he is also a therapist, based in the north of England. Philip embodies Britishness: speaking in a measured manner, with particularly precise pronunciation. My accent-related shame resurfaces instantly, although I thought it had receded years ago.

"Why have you decided to talk with me instead of someone locally?" I shoot straight away.

"I actually like the fact that you are not from here. And it

229

matters to me that you nevertheless understand my culture." He needs no time to reflect, confirming that he had thought about this thoroughly beforehand.

Now that Philip's image is clearer on my screen, I can look at him properly. He fits well with my idea of a retired provincial headmaster, well mannered and composed, or even a priest.

"Before I trained as a therapist, I worked as a law-enforcement officer." He totally dispels my fantasy.

He then tells me about his work at a therapy clinic for the last twenty years, the long walks with his dogs across the fields that surround the farm he lives on. Philip recites all this as a well-learnt part from a well-prepared actor playing a therapy patient.

"What brings you here today?" I ask.

"I dreaded this question," he exhales with a disarming honesty, which makes me instantly like him.

We sit in silence, considering his fear and his confusion. His square face, creased with deep lines all over, remains strangely shut, and his dark gaze is wandering elsewhere. I can tell that he is not used to translating his own feelings into words. It takes him a long moment to utter: "I am lost."

As he finally looks at me, I can see agony in his eyes.

"When did you start feeling this way?"

"I don't know ... it happened gradually. I kept trying to focus on work, on resolving other people's problems, you know," a fleeting smile crosses his face. "But nothing makes much sense anymore."

I get his irony. Bearing in mind that Philip is a colleague, his existential struggle resonates with particular intensity. If the loss of meaning is a major issue for anybody, for a therapist it can turn into a nightmarish experience. Being constantly exposed to human dramas, therapists are vulnerable to this blight. Therapy is a meaning-making activity; a therapist in loss of meaning becomes inept.

Philip

"How do you cope with your work?"

"I mostly don't anymore," he acknowledges and looks away.

Philip's practice has been dying slowly, and the lockdown dealt it a final blow.

"At the beginning I kept meeting with a few clients over the phone, but now there is only one left who still turns up … She is probably too depressed and embarrassed to end it," he concludes with a barely disguised relief.

"What about your family?"

He just shrugs at my question, and it takes us another while to get to the bottom of his despair. His wife left him the year before to move in with their neighbour, and his life has been shrinking further, as he isolated himself, out of embarrassment and pain. As the pandemic forced the village pub to close down, he lost his last connection with the outside world.

"I don't even know what I am hoping for," he says looking at me with dismay. "I am sorry to inflict this onto you …"

My heart goes out to him, and the words pour out of my mouth without pre-meditation. "Please, do not. Your lostness is also mine, and anybody else's for that matter … Just human, right?"

He smiles again, this time for a split second longer. Or maybe this is what I wish to believe.

We agree on giving it a go, and when I switch off, 'remote and rural' keeps coming back to me. I imagine him pouring himself a large glass of whisky after talking with me, dismayed at the closed pub and his own existence, the emptiness of which has only been highlighted further by the stormy night and the lockdown.

Something in Philip's not fitting in with his world resonates with me. Will I be able to capitalise on this resonance and help him reclaim his life?

***

Our second session does not take place as planned. Philip cancels with the excuse of a medical appointment for which he must drive to the next town. I find myself not believing him. I imagine his lonely figure, flanked by his old dogs (which I picture as some sort of terriers), walking on the cliffs. Or is he drinking silently in his dark cottage, swept by endless winter rains? I write back, mimicking his polite British tone, offering to reschedule. All through the day, as I see other clients, an uneasy feeling keeps rattling me from inside: I know Philip is unwell.

The next day, still without a reply from him, I pick up the phone and dial the number that he put in his succinctly filled form. The signal is there, and the ringing sounds 'remote and rural', exactly like Philip himself. I leave a message, truthfully saying that I am concerned about him and ask him to get in touch.

In the evening Philip finally calls back: "Sorry I missed your call. I was on the cliffs with the dogs … I would actually like to meet as soon as possible … if you are still ok with seeing me, of course."

***

This time, the first thing I hear is dogs barking. Philip's image is coming up slowly, I see him standing up, leaving the room and scolding the dogs – two overly excited fox terriers actively resisting eviction from the room.

"I am sorry. Now they are used to spending most of the time outside …"

It takes Philip a few long minutes to sort the dogs out before we can properly begin.

"I am sorry I called yesterday … I usually don't," I recognise, slightly uneasy about what could have looked like chasing him.

"You are very intuitive …," he smiles sadly. "I probably have to tell you this. I don't want to put you through anything unpleasant …"

Philip

Now he has piqued my curiosity: "What do you mean?"

He keeps avoiding my eyes, which isn't too difficult through the screen, and keeps me hanging for a long minute. I wait.

"The doctor's appointment was an excuse ... I just do not believe in therapy anymore," he looks devastated by his own words.

I have heard this line several times before, but never from a therapist.

"Why did you contact me in the first place then?"

"Good question. I don't really know. On a whim, I suppose. Stumbled on your blog ... something resonated ... But it was a mistake. I don't think I can do this."

"Philip, I am sorry but I have already accepted you as a client. And we are talking today, again. We both know the rules. I cannot force you to do this ... but let's give it a last chance today, shall we?"

Now I feel really challenged. I will not let him give up. My own inner fox terrier is now alerted.

He looks at his screen, finally, but does not respond, so I give him the last push: "OK, let's make a deal. No playing around. You talk honestly today, just doing what you expect your clients to do, and then you can decide if you want to leave it there,"

"OK. Deal," he finally exhales, and I am not sure whether he is annoyed or relieved.

We both take a deep breath and start all over again.

"Yesterday I went to the cliffs to kill myself," he announces, embracing my challenge.

As soon as these words leave his mouth, I can finally feel my guts relaxing.

"I am glad you did not," I say simply.

"Yes, that would be a shit situation for you to handle. A client who commits suicide after the first session."

Fair analysis.

"What stopped you then?" I am not ready to let him off the hook. Peeking at the clock in the right corner of my screen, I realise that we have only forty minutes left.

"Cowardice …" he retorts with disdain " … and your call. You can be happy," he adds angrily.

"I am happy. But are you cross with me?"

"I am cross with myself."

"Any particular reason?"

"I just keep letting people down."

"People?"

"My wife … ex-wife … Eventually everybody who crosses my path."

"You maybe have let some people down. But not everybody. Not me. By not jumping off that cliff you made sure you didn't." This is a long shot, but I have to try. Our relationship is yet too little, too fragile to be enough to pull him back to firmer ground; I must buy some time to allow it to grow.

He shrugs dismissively, his lips shut tight.

I sense him still perching at the very edge of that cliff. And there is not much holding him back apart from the two dogs – no children, no wife, not even clients. I glance at the clock again – thirty-eight minutes left. I absolutely have to find somebody or something in his life that is meaningful enough to keep him alive.

"Philip, could we go together through the list of people who you have let down?"

He is not thrilled with this prospect, but nods.

"Where should we start? Childhood?" I offer almost lightly.

He sighs, but a deal is a deal. This time I catch him looking sideways at his computer clock – thirty-five minutes remaining.

"I grew up in a small town, just a few miles away from here …," he stumbles on the very first sentence, retreating into his dark bubble again.

"Another remote and rural place?" I try to make him start.

"Pretty much so," he agrees. "My two parents were Londoners, but came here to teach at the local grammar school ... I always felt like a square peg in a round hole, if you see what I mean."

"I do," I confirm, and this is not just about the English expression. Not fitting in was my reality too – and, even today, the feeling of shame about being foreign or somehow 'bizarre' still catches up with me sometimes.

"I was just different from the other kids; too awkward to play their games. I was never invited in and would mostly spend time with adults or alone ..."

Philip's parents were teaching at his school, and other kids resented him for the particular status it gave him. He was a bright, curious kid; teachers often put him forward as an example for others, without thinking too much about how this would affect his integration into the school. His parents, absorbed by their vocation, never invited other boys to their house, either to protect their privacy or out of secret disdain for the poorer kids who lived in local council houses.

"This all sounds very lonely," I try to remind Philip that I am still here, listening to his story, and this is not meant to be a monologue.

"I was lonely, I suppose," he recognises reluctantly.

"My impression is that *you* were let down by the grown-ups," I suggest.

"And yet I constantly felt that I was letting everybody down – other boys because I did not run fast enough to catch the ball, my parents because I was not interested enough in their subjects or not able to make friends."

His father taught maths and his mother sciences. Passionate about their careers, they showed no interest in anything Philip was attracted to – books, poetry and drama. They did not like his success in artistic subjects which they perceived as unimportant.

"One day I did not win the school competition in maths and my father said something that stayed with me forever … No matter how many times I've recounted this in therapy, those words have never left me: 'You are the biggest disappointment of my life!'"

"Ouch, that is cruel," I utter, as there is no need to repeat what Philip has certainly heard before. "What a terrible thing to say to your child."

"My father wanted me to become a headmaster," he adds with remorse.

"But you did not."

"No, I didn't. As soon as I finished school I applied to enrol on a police apprenticeship. My parents were devastated, as they had high hopes for their only child."

"Why the police then?"

"That was the only way I could find to leave the town and start earning money straight away … Maybe I also wanted to hurt them."

For the following three years Philip's life was dominated by calls to neighbouring villages to deal with things like a fight in a pub or domestic violence. During those days he often felt 'out of place' again, made no friends with other police officers, but the idea of making the world a better place kept him going. Proving to his parents that he had made the right choice also played a role in his stubborn path towards probation, then qualification, and finally to what looked at the time as a promising career in the police.

"But after a few years I started feeling completely disconnected … I went around doing my duty like a zombie, really … That is when I started going to the pub."

"What happened?"

"I was just exposed to too much human misery … too much

human ugliness, I suppose."

"And you were still very lonely ..."

"I was ... and also all these evenings at the pub ... my drinking was running wild."

Philip was steadily sinking into what only later he could identify as depression. "But at the time I thought that I should probably just work a little harder, maybe find a girlfriend, start a family ..."

Philip seems completely back to his past, from which the same sadness emanates as from his present life.

"Nothing, not even saving the vulnerable and punishing the bad, was making sense anymore."

"Just like now."

"I guess," he admits sadly.

"Is it when you decided to train to become a therapist?"

"No, not really ... I didn't even know it was an option. Asking for support is not something widely discussed among police officers; therapy is considered to be for victims, for the abused and the assaulted," he says with bitter irony.

"Do you still believe that?"

My question takes him aback. "You know what? I probably do."

"So, what brought you to therapy?"

"A woman ..." he stops short of telling me more, as his whole face lights up. A sudden sunny patch has just appeared in the middle of the heavy grey sky.

A dog's loud barking make us both glance at the clock.

"We probably should end anyway," he confirms sardonically. I have to agree, although this is not the best moment. I am relieved to hear some energy in his voice, but is it enough to keep him away from that cliff?

"You should tell me about her next time ... What is her name by the way?"

"Emily," he exhales faintly.

Impatient, the fox terriers are now scratching at the door.

"Sorry, I will have to let them in. Time for the evening walk," he explains unapologetically and leaves his desk. I watch him opening the door and the two dogs jumping excitedly around him.

When Philip returns to his seat, the dogs join him there, flanking him on both sides, tongues out, looking at me whimsically.

"You do know that you have to promise me to be there next week?" I try to seal a pact.

He nods. "I will not kill myself before our Tuesday session," he repeats somehow mockingly, and I badly want to believe him.

Alone in my office, I secretly hope that the ray of sunshine at the end of that session will help protect Philip from himself. He is stubbornly playing both Scheherazade and King Shahryar who wants her dead. The silver lining may be that, by letting me step in, he gives us an opportunity to change something in his downward spiral.

The image of the fox terriers, wandering on top of the deserted cliff, howling in search of their master, lingers in my mind for the next few days. It also returns in the night, as one morning I wake up with my heart racing, a distinct feeling of dread. I resist calling him; I want to trust his promise. Philip has to tell the rest of his story. I am embracing the heavy weight of his timid trust with that painful humility that our profession comes with.

***

When Philip's face, out-of-focus but alive, returns to my screen, the knot that has been nestling in my stomach finally unwinds.

"Glad to see you again," I greet him, and he smiles, acknowledging my relief with the usual sarcastic grimace.

"Not sure I'm as thrilled as you are," he glances at the corner of his screen, where his sad face would be flickering. "But still hanging around."

"At least one of us is happy about that," I insist, making his features lighten up for a split second, with one of those melancholy smiles that I am starting to seek out.

"I guess I now have to tell you about Emily." In the best Scheherazade tradition he picks up exactly where we left it the previous time. "She was the purpose and the light of my life for a long time."

As I let the weight of his words sink in, he retreats. "This probably sounds heavy ... heavier than I intended."

"It also sounds sincere," I argue.

"I suppose it is," he consents. "I'd better tell you the whole story then ..."

I agree.

"I was twenty-eight and spiralling down, demotivated by my work. I was drinking most evenings, often alone ... This is when I met Emily. She was bartending then at a pub I liked a few miles away from the village where I lived."

Emily was nineteen then and probably more lost than Philip himself. When they first made out after her long night shift, they were both quite a few drinks in. But as inebriated as he was, Philip felt instantly concerned about her. There was something intolerably fragile about Emily, her thin body, her surprisingly black hair, her translucent grey eyes. "She looked as if she was from a different planet, really ..."

She stayed over that night, and only seeing her naked in the cruel morning light, he realised how young she actually was. Her colourless skin showed her veins and she was covered with scars and bruises that she made no attempt to conceal. There was nothing sexual in what Philip felt looking at her, but rather a yearning to protect her, to shield her from the cruelties of their cold surroundings. And this yearning was irresistible.

"That same morning she asked me if she could stay with me … She offered to clean my house, to do chores. She was desperate for a roof over her head. I could not wish for anything better. It took her a few weeks and several drinks to tell me why. Her father was a real bastard. He beat her mother routinely, and Emily had had to put up with his abuse for years. At that time things were getting worse as her mother had been admitted to a psychiatric hospital after a suicide attempt … Emily knew I was a cop and this made her feel safe."

This is when Philip took Emily under his wing, and after just a few months they got married. "She literally saved me from my desperate loneliness. We kind of anchored each other, and it worked for a while …"

The marks on her body faded quickly, but those on her mind and soul, less visible, turned out to be harder to heal.

"She drank often, self-harmed from time to time, and regularly retreated into a kind of inner dark room in which she would punish herself for being a bad person, a bad wife. There was no way of approaching her then, she would hiss like a feral cat, ready to scratch or bite. I quickly learnt to stay away …"

She would sleep on the sofa for several nights in a row, imposing a kind of solitary confinement on herself and her husband. Philip did as well as he could to keep them both afloat but, even if caring for Emily gave him a purpose, the responsibility was overwhelming.

"One day I came back from work to find her lying on the floor, barely breathing …" Even thirty-five years later, Philip stumbles on his own words; the images that they awaken are still too painful.

"She was rushed to hospital and stayed in a coma for three

weeks ... I sat there and watched her dying ..."

The dogs' barking interrupts Philip's tale again, forcing him to stop in the middle of a sentence. The door-bell rings melodically a few times, but Philip does not move from his chair, ignoring the commotion happening on the other side of his locked door.

"Would you like to check what is going on at your door?" I offer, as the dogs keep barking excitedly.

"No, I wouldn't," he responds with defiance.

"You know who that is, don't you?"

"I do," he confirms.

We sit for a few long minutes, peering at each other, listening to the dogs' frantic barking. When the fox terriers finally calm down, I am still waiting for some explanation. But it does not come.

"Our time is up," Philip says with a perfidious smile instead.

Unfortunately he is right and this time I feel a little more confident about leaving him until the next time. Talking about Emily has brought some energy into the room. As long as Philip has more to tell me about her, he will probably keep going. I still do not know whether Emily is still alive, but I can tell that she holds the power to keep him away from that cliff.

***

"Once out of the hospital, she ended up on the sofa again and stayed there for days with no desire or ability to move." Philip resumes his tale as if a week had not passed since our last session. He actually wears the same checked, rusty brown shirt and his face displays the same disquietude. Has he not even left this room for a week, I wonder.

I would prefer to connect with Philip somehow in the 'here-and-now' of this shared moment, but I let go of this passing thought and bite my tongue as he keeps narrating his story. Having me as a witness for the struggles he shared with Emily seems to be what he needs right now.

"I didn't know what to do, did not know where to ask for help … until a counsellor came to check on her … She was one of those ageless ladies in a beige raincoat … And looking at her, I first thought 'no way will Emily talk to her'. When she saw the state of things (our house was a total mess by then) and Emily lying on the sofa surrounded by empty boxes of cheap wine, she took control."

The counsellor did exactly what a mother or any sensitive adult would have done at the sight of two troubled kids left alone. She helped Philip to clean the kitchen, made tea, talked to Emily who, bewildered by this sudden intrusion, listened … Before leaving, she gave them details of Alcoholics Anonymous meetings and promised to come back the following week to drive Emily there.

"Sounds like she knew exactly what she was doing," I can barely resist saying.

"She was a blessing indeed. She kept coming for a while, home visits were a rare commodity even then …"

"This is so different from what we are doing here, isn't it?" I state the obvious, making an attempt to bring him back into our shared present moment.

"This whole online therapy thing is just …," he stops short from naming his true feelings and looks at me with unease, suddenly aware of my flimsy presence on his screen.

"I would also prefer to be in the same room as you," I admit "but this is what we have, so why not try to make it work for you?"

"I am too old for this," he replies grumpily, looking elsewhere.

"Philip, I know that what I have to offer right now is far less than what that counsellor did for you two at the time … but in some strange way I am also there with you, in your cottage. I certainly cannot do your dishes but maybe, if only you let us try, we can reinvent the miracle that counselling was able to do for you and Emily back then?"

"What for? Emily is not here anymore and does not seem to need any miracles from me."

"Would you like to tell me more about what happened after that counsellor came into your lives?"

"No. I do not want to talk about my marriage anymore," he suddenly announces in a surprising U-turn from his previous narrative strategy. As I absorb this new rule that Philip sets, he remains silent. What I can see of his body on my screen is so still that for a second I wonder whether the connection has been lost.

"What would you like to talk about instead?"

"I do not want to talk. I feel like I have used all the words I had."

"Do you mean words about Emily?"

"Yes," he admits and looks annoyed.

I suddenly feel a wave of anger mounting in me. This is the first time I feel irritated with Philip. Surprised by this realisation, I follow his example and keep silent.

Philip has now come out of his stillness and fidgets in his chair.

"Are you angry with Emily?" I make a guess; this abrupt wave of anger seems to be coming from his side of the screen.

"Am I angry?" he considers my question for a second. "I am actually furious!"

As soon as he acknowledges this, my own anger is replaced by curiosity.

"Why?"

"She left me. After thirty years, she just walked away. And you know where she went? She just crossed the street to move in with Roger!"

"Who is Roger?" Now I am eager to know more.

"Our blooming doctor."

I am thrilled to see Philip fuming, appreciating the energy that anger brings into his body, into our virtual room. His face, lifeless until now, lights up and lets me see something that I have not seen before – he certainly used to be a very attractive man.

"We used to be good neighbours. I trusted him. We built a fence together, like good friends"

The double betrayal that he has to deal with fills him with shame.

"He was our GP for years. He saw me naked. Touched my throat glands ...," he shivers in disgust.

"This is so hurtful ... I am so sorry." The only words I can find are too little of course.

"I didn't see it coming ... What a fool I was!"

"Philip, there is nothing foolish in love. You loved Emily and you lost her. This is the risk we all take in giving our heart away to someone. Emily loved you too. You loved each other for thirty years ... It's an accomplishment."

"But she spoiled it all. How could she?" Struggling with the break-up, Philip looks young and vulnerable.

"Did she explain her reasons for walking away?"

"She tried. What a pitiful attempt to justify her cheating on me .... And of all people in the world she chose this ..." In a superhuman effort, Philip swallows back the insult burning his lips. From the pained grimace that follows I see that it keeps burning him further down his throat, and then in his chest which he brushes in a futile attempt to chase the pain away.

"So what did she say?"

"She said that she was bored with our life and that we had been together for too long, saving each other from misery initially, but she did not need to be saved anymore and wanted to enjoy what remained of her life."

Philip

Philip stares at me, expecting me to join him in his indignation. As I look at the ageing man on my screen, I can figure out why Emily decided to leave him. She must be in her early fifties now, sober, healthy and active, if I understood correctly from what Philip has told me so far about her. With his heavy frame, dishevelled hair and grumpy smirk, Philip looks worn down, older than his early sixties.

"I understand that her words have been very hurtful … but is there anything in what she said that can make sense?"

With his anger gone, Philip now looks deflated again.

"We had been saving each other from misery indeed," he says sadly. "But now that she is gone, I feel more miserable than ever, while she seems just fine."

"How do you know? Have you spoken since her departure?"

"No, I don't want to see her. I just can't."

"Was it her, ringing the doorbell during our last session?"

He nods, confirming his stubborn refusal to let her in again.

"Philip, what is your plan then? Avoiding her forever? It seems a bit difficult if you live on the same street."

"My plan, until I met you, was to end it all," he responds angrily again.

"If this really was your plan, you probably would not have contacted me, would you?"

He does not answer and I already regret saying that.

"Philip, I am really glad you reached out, we can help you out of this dark place."

"You cannot make her come back, can you?"

"No, I cannot," I admit the limitations of therapy. "But I can help you achieve many other things."

"What, for example? Making us be friends?" he suggests with bitter irony.

245

"Would you like that?" I ask.

"This is pathetic. We are not kids, for God's sake!"

"I do not find friendship pathetic. Emily has apparently been trying to reconnect and talk ... She probably cares for you more than you think," I say, hoping that this is not wishful thinking on my part.

"She's come every single day. She leaves food by the door ... How ridiculous!"

"And you have never opened the door?"

"No ... And the food goes directly in the bin," he admits stubbornly.

"This is a little puerile, don't you think?"

"Maybe," he concedes, "but I cannot talk to her ... It is too painful. Not yet."

I like hearing his 'not yet'; maybe we are moving in the right direction. Confronting Emily is a necessary step for Philip to resume his life.

"Let's talk about it next week," I conclude, slightly more comfortable with leaving him alone this time.

***

The space around Philip is dark; his face, dimly lit by a desk lamp, looks uncertain and slightly blurred. In a striking contrast, a glorious sun has been shining into my office from the window, forcing me to roll the blinds down just before the session. The newly arrived spring is blissfully unaware of another round of pandemic restrictions.

"It's very dark in that room – are you hiding?" I ask bluntly hoping to dig him out of his shame retreat. His self-imposed isolation is not dissimilar to Emily's staying on the sofa for days of self-punishment. At least Philip looks sober.

"The shutters are closed," he announces.

"Would you like to take a moment and open them?" It is still early morning in England, but Philip is an early riser, and when he connected from other rooms in his house for our previous sessions, there was sunlight.

"I don't open them anymore ... I haven't since she left," he admits, and then adds reluctantly: "I cannot bear the sight of that house ..."

"Do you mean Roger's house?"

He nods in disdain. "I haven't been using the front door either."

"How do you get in and out of the house then?"

"From the back door," he replies with embarrassment. "I haven't been in the garden either."

Since his wife left, Philip has restricted his life to the bare minimum, depriving himself of anything that could provide him any joy – gardening, proper meals, or – as his looks may suggest – even a shower. If it were not for the dogs, he probably would not even leave the house.

"Are you punishing yourself for not making Emily happy for ever?"

"I may be," he seems taken aback by this hypothesis.

"But is it fair? You helped her out of depression and addiction, and made her reasonably happy for three decades. Isn't that enough?"

He shrugs.

"Philip, losing Emily has been terribly painful for you, but do you really have to lose everything else as well?"

"Probably not," he hums, and I retain a smile.

"So, why don't we start with opening these shutters and let some sunshine in?"

"The house is too messy anyway," he resists weakly.

"I can close my eyes," I finally smile.

With a sigh he stands up and exits my screen. I can hear him shuffling about and the dogs' claws on the wooden floor sound like they are following him. The shutters' hinges creak and sunlight breaks into Philip's living room. It looks surprisingly cosy, with warm colours and large bookshelves filled with books and knick-knacks.

When he returns, Philip looks remorseful. "Emily's plants are dead … She would be devastated," he comments. And indeed, the two massive ficus plants that I can now spot in the corner of the room look desperately thirsty, with a few dry leaves still hanging here and there, like sleeping bats.

"You could water them, maybe it is not too late," I suggest.

He smirks, but somehow I know he will do it.

"I keep imagining them looking at me from the window and laughing," Philip goes back to what has been bothering him.

"Do you mean Emily and Roger? Why are you so sure they are making fun of you?"

"What else do you want them to laugh about? They made me a perfect laughing stock."

The sound of the doorbell interrupts Philip's speech, instantly sending him into panic. I silently hope it is Emily, trying her luck again. Will I be able to see her this time?

"She saw me opening the shutters! Now she knows I am inside." He freezes in his chair, looks at me with reproach and blurts: "What should I do now?!"

"What about opening the door and seeing what she has to say?"

"No, I will not," he pounds, leaving no space for discussion.

We sit in silence for a few long minutes as the doorbell keeps ringing and the dogs are going absolutely nuts, barking and running in and out of the room, in a desperate attempt to bring their master back to his senses. Once the doorbell finally falls silent, the fox terriers keep yelping and racing around.

"Wait a second, I have to calm them down before they drive me crazy." Philip leaves me alone again.

When he returns, with the dogs following him closely, there is an envelope in his hands. "She left a letter," he announces and sits down, both dogs joining him on the sofa, sniffing the envelope excitedly.

"They have been missing Emily," he pats them tenderly, as I have not seen him doing before. It seems easier for Philip to acknowledge his dogs' hurt feelings rather than his own.

"Probably not as much as you have," I add. "Would you like to open the letter now?"

He puts the envelope down on the desk as a precious but dangerous object. "I am not sure I want to read this."

"What are you afraid it may contain?"

"I don't know ... Divorce papers?"

"Philip, the only way to find out is to open it. The question is – would you like to read it here and now, with me?"

He considers my question for a moment then repeats stubbornly: "I don't want to read it."

I want to know more about Emily's letter and, surely, so does Philip. But therapy has very little to do with television series: twists and cliff-hangers only rarely lead to a neat resolution. Therapists' days overflow with frustrations of every kind: clients make little or no progress, resist the obvious truth, stumble on self-created obstacles and sometimes simply drop off prematurely.

This time I must settle on an unopened letter, respecting Philip's choice. Facing his wife's truth is still too much to take on. Apart from Philip's broken heart, we must deal with his existential crisis. My guess is that the two are intertwined more than he is willing to acknowledge.

"Philip, as you imagine Emily and Roger laughing at you, what do you think they may be saying?"

"I don't know … and I don't care."

"Could you just share your thoughts?"

He seems torn between his desire to get better and the temptation to switch me off by clicking the red 'end' button on his screen. Finally he opts for playing along. "They may be saying something about me being lazy, worthless … useless," he finally puts words on his shame.

"Is it something that Emily ever said to you?"

"No … apart from the 'lazy' part, I guess. She always complained that I didn't help enough around the house," he admits, slightly embarrassed.

"So, where do the 'worthless and useless' come from then?"

"My father …? Myself? I do feel useless. Before, Emily needed me badly … Then my clients needed me as much, sometimes even more. But now all that is gone. Apart from my dogs I guess nobody needs me at all."

The only way he ever managed to feel worthy was by dedicating himself to helping others, as a police officer, a husband or a therapist. With the pandemic, the clinic where Philip met his clients has had to close down, and as he stubbornly resisted moving his practice online, he has now found himself with no clear purpose for the first time in years. His life has lost any meaning.

"That is why I hate Roger. He is so full of purpose. The other day I heard from the neighbours that he has gone back to the hospital, volunteering with the NHS to save lives … A true hero!" The disdain in his voice hardly covers Philip's shame – a thin layer of transparent ice on the murky waters of a bottomless pond. And now we are staggering on this paper-thin ice together.

"Have you considered doing the same?"

"Who needs me?" The anger in his voice can barely cover the hurt.

"Philip, medical doctors and nurses do need counselling right now. More than ever."

"But I cannot just go there and push my dubious counselling skills onto them, can I?"

"Surely you can find a way to volunteer to work with front-line medical staff," I suggest and resist crossing my fingers under the desk. I can almost hear the ice crack.

"Does it mean that I have to do this … online thing?"

"Why not? You have been doing 'this online thing' with me for a while after all …"

"I don't know if I can do it," he resists with no conviction.

"If you can do this as a client, I do not see why you could not do it as a therapist," I take a short cut.

I leave him there, with his empty screen and the letter from his wife on the desk, both items waiting for him to take a plunge.

***

"I couldn't do it," he announces defiantly – a bad student fearing his teacher's scolding.

Every time I see a colleague as a client, I am sent back to my own therapy on the other side of the screen. Philip is the barefoot child of the cobbler. Although I can easily imagine him empathic and non-judgemental with his clients, he is uncharitable with himself.

"Philip, I was not expecting you to immediately follow up on my advice," I'm exaggerating and he can certainly spot it. "Or at least, not straightaway." Tactful, he lets my clumsiness go unremarked.

"I saw Emily in the street the other day … She looked happy

… With me, she rarely was."

"Did she see you?"

"No, I hid behind the bushes," he says, clearly aware of the childishness of his behaviour.

"For how long do you plan to play this hide-and-seek?"

"I don't know … I am wondering whether I made her unhappy for all these years."

"Philip, you are heart-broken and probably not clear headed about her feelings. I think it is time to let her tell you in her own words what she means, don't you think?"

"Do you want me to read her letter then?" he asks, too exhausted to resist the obvious.

"If you are ready."

He picks up the envelope that has stayed on his desk since last time and gently opens it. His face slowly transforms into a white mask, free from any expression. From the moment he starts reading, he forgets about my virtual presence. It takes him several long minutes to go through the letter and somewhere halfway, tears start coming down his cheeks. A part of me would prefer to leave him alone but I also want to be there when he is ready to process what Emily has to say.

When he finally puts the letter away and looks at me, his face is dry and blank – a city devastated by a storm.

"She is in love," he confirms.

"Is that all?"

"No … She also says that I will always be the biggest love of her life and that without me she would never have survived."

I want to ask the obvious question: "Why Roger then?" but keep quiet.

Philip continues: "But she saw me as more of a friend to her, not a lover anymore."

Philip

He is certainly not the first abandoned spouse confused by such a statement. I have not much of an explanation to offer. Romantic passions are flimsy companions. As Emily grew older and evolved in the security of their relationship, she developed other needs that Philip was not ready to satisfy. Roger lived just across the street. He was available, with plenty of free time since his retirement and, most importantly, he was different.

"Roger has never seen me drunk or depressed, he never cleaned up my vomit. For him I am the woman I am today. You loved my struggle and needed me to be fragile to feel strong and worthy," now Philip reads from the letter, and this time his face isn't blank. His voice cracks, as rage is starting to come through the pain.

"That isn't very fair, is it?" I add oil to the fire.

"I cannot believe that is how she sees it!"

"Philip, Emily is in love and sounds appropriately blind."

"She discarded me like an old tissue, now that I am of no use to her anymore."

"Philip, if you are of no use to her, this does not mean that you are useless," I say hoping that he appreciates the point.

"I will just go and punch this bastard in his face," he groans.

Philip's fist hits the desk, making his computer bounce. All things being equal, I prefer him smashing the furniture rather than his neighbour's face.

"Philip, you are angry ..."

"I have not felt this furious in years!" he admits, staring at his fist in bewilderment.

"What do you usually do when you are angry?"

"I used to drink ... or get in a fight ... but that was a long time ago."

Philip's anger gives him a burst of energy that had deserted his life. I want to make the most of this opportunity, to break the stillness of his depression.

"Are there other ways of showing Emily and Roger that you are neither worthless nor useless?"

"You want me to volunteer with the NHS, don't you?"

I nod. There is no reason to pretend I do not.

"You are really stubborn, aren't you?"

I nod again. He got this right too.

"You may be right. I am fed up sitting around and watching the depressing news."

This is where I leave him, hoping that this time he will be able to act.

***

When I see Philip again, on his side of the screen the setting is very different. He is now wearing a plain blue sweater with a neat white shirt underneath. His face is clear on the screen and brightly lit sideways by sunlight through the window. He also looks anxious.

"I read some advice on the internet about conducting sessions online. Is the light ok?"

"It is," I confirm, smiling at his transition – from an online client to an online therapist.

"I have got my first referral from the charity … It's a medical doctor. I see him tomorrow."

Philip has not taken on a new client in months now, and this is the very first time he is seeing one on video without meeting in person beforehand.

"What if the call drops out? What if I cannot hear what he is saying?" Philip has many questions and we spend the rest of the session talking about online therapy, discussing its potential pitfalls, its unexpected advantages.

"What if he does not find this online thing helpful?"

"This online thing?"

"Online therapy, I mean. What if he finds it useless?"

"Are you afraid this doctor will find *you* useless, as you think Emily did?"

He nods and I am touched by how vulnerable he is allowing himself to be.

"Philip, do you find online therapy useless?"

"No, I don't. It has actually been very helpful to talk with you," he acknowledges for the first time.

"So, can we imagine for a second that this overworked and stressed doctor will also find it beneficial?"

Philip agrees silently, but looks unconvinced.

"Can we talk this through again after the first session?"

"That would be great."

Strictly speaking, this is turning into supervision rather than therapy, a different type of work, a different kind of relationship, but this is what seems most helpful to Philip right now. After all, in his life, he has rarely got his own needs met and this is an opportunity to reverse this damaging pattern.

"Thank you," he says wholeheartedly before leaving my screen.

***

"I cannot believe that bastard did this to me!"

Our next session, which I expected to be a smooth supervisory run, starts in a completely different manner. Philip looks at me in confusion – a child disappointed by his long-expected birthday gift. The scruffy checked shirt is back, and the screen is unstable again. Philip is fuming.

"Could you tell me a little more?"

"He pretended to be somebody else, can you even imagine that?!"

"Who are you talking about?"

"Roger," he spits out in his most disdainful tone.

Now it is my turn to look at him in bewilderment.

"He saw my name on the list of therapists that was given to the hospital by the charity. He used the name of another doctor to book a session."

"Roger went a long way to talk to you, didn't he?"

"Manipulative bastard."

"You had been shutting him down for weeks."

"He said he was worried about me! Him. Worried. About me."

"Might he not be after all?"

"After stealing my wife, he surely feels guilty."

"Possibly indeed but this does not mean he is not genuinely worried for you ... You used to be friends."

Philip turns away from the screen in an attempt to hide his tears. Not only has seeing Roger shaken him, but also the way Roger engineered the encounter feels like another betrayal.

It takes me the rest of the session to help Philip report on their conversation. Roger talked about how he had been drawn to Emily for years but resisted the attraction until Emily herself came to his garden one day and bluntly declared her feelings: "We both know how she is when she puts her mind to getting something ..." Philip was tempted to cut their 'session' short a few times, but then Roger spoke about Emily with such tenderness that he could not help thinking that he had never loved her in such an absolute and sincere way.

"I never saw in her what he is able to see," he recognises with disbelief. "At some point I almost thought he was talking about another woman ... one I have never met."

Roger also talked about his work back at the hospital. He was assigned to the emergency room, where he had not been since his medical training. Understaffed in normal times, the small country hospital has been completely overwhelmed with the wave of Covid patients. But despite the stress and fatigue, Roger felt 'energised and humbled' by this challenge.

"You know, I felt envious of his energy …," Philip confesses reluctantly.

Despite his anger and hurt, he could also see what Emily saw in Roger. Now, after witnessing his rival's superiority, he felt worse, belittled and ashamed of his own inactivity and his recent plans to end his life while Roger was fighting to save lives.

"He is the big man, and I am the small one, so pathetic …"

"Philip, I can see that talking with Roger was a humbling experience, but I also notice that this 'big man' has been fighting to gain back your friendship. He cares enough for you to take the risk of usurping a colleague's identity just to reach you."

"He asked if we could meet for another 'session' …" he says in a barely audible voice.

"Will you see him?"

Philip shakes his head in a way that leaves space for interpretation. I do not want to press him further; he probably needs time to deal with this dilemma.

***

Soon Philip and I settle into a weekly routine. Each time he updates me on his most recent 'session' with Roger, creating the uncanny effect of a parallel therapy, in which the two men are finally able to confront each other. They both find solace in reconnecting in the virtual bubble that these online encounters provide them. They feel strangely 'safe' in front of their respective computers, physically distant by just a hundred metres and a small street. In 'real life' they keep avoiding each other and, if their paths cross by chance at the village shop or the post office, they simply pretend to be vague acquaintances exchanging a rushed 'hello' and moving on with their days, until their next online session, where they find intimacy and become confidants again.

During that 'therapy', I witness their friendship growing stronger and deeper. From one session to another, I observe the healing process unfolding. Philip does not talk much about forgiveness, but we both recognise that these conversations are repairing something deeper in him, with Roger generously mirroring Philip's doubts, making him feel valuable and alive again.

"I cannot believe I am having this secret friendship with the man who took my wife," he would often say half-jokingly. "What is wrong with me?"

Philip is always quick to doubt about himself and this question is constantly present in the background of our conversations, like a soundtrack for his shame.

"Well, there is nothing wrong with friendship, is there?" I keep on challenging his self-deprecating views.

Slowly, over several months, Philip resumes seeing patients. Our screen sessions and his on-going talks with Roger make him feel more confident with communicating online and in general.

I start to believe that their reuniting 'for real' is only a matter of time. I have some kind of fantasy about Philip accepting an invitation to Roger's house for a meal. When we discuss it, he retreats, reluctant to re-engage at the same time with both of them.

"I cannot see Emily ... Not there, not with him," he explains. Meeting Roger somewhere other than in the slightly surreal screen setting would still feel 'humiliating'.

***

"He didn't show up," Philip announces at the start of our

session. He looks troubled again. For a few months, neither of them had missed a 'session'.

"Did he write to you?"

"No, nothing. He just wasn't there. I waited for half an hour in front of the screen, like an idiot."

"Have you tried to reach him?" I wonder as Philip's anxiety is quickly filling the space between us, making any other conversation impossible.

As he is considering this idea in silence, the dogs that have been peacefully lying on the sofa, jump up, agitated and run out of the room barking.

"Wait a second," Philip announces and follows them. I am left in front of his empty room again, with an uncanny sense of déjà-vu. I hear a door opening, faint voices, the door closing again.

This time he returns empty handed.

"Roger got Covid, he's hospitalised," Philip's voice is as blank as his face. "Emily has just come round to tell me the news".

***

"He managed to depart like a hero, the bastard," Philip attempts a sad smile despite tears filling up his eyes.

He went to see his rival at the hospital. Roger was put on a ventilator, which made any talking impossible. Philip, wearing full PPE, sat on a plastic chair by his bed for a few minutes, before the nurse asked him to leave.

"I told him that I was glad that this time he had to shut up and listen to what I had to say. I knew he did not want me to cry. I did not. I told him that I forgave him and that I was grateful for his friendship. He saved my life like he saved many others. He was crying and I was standing there like an alien in that horrid white suit ... I could not even hug him or take his hand."

Roger died a few days later from pulmonary complications.

Philip organised his Covid-compliant burial together with Emily. Their shared grief brought them closer. Their relationship resumed under a brand-new form, as different from their marriage years as a fully formed colourful butterfly would be from the pre-metamorphosis larva. She stayed in Roger's house, kept taking care of his garden, and they often talked standing on each side of the fence that Philip and Roger had built together.

***

Facing one's shame and recognising its terrifying grasp on one's life is often the biggest challenge in therapy. It is also one of the major opportunities a therapeutic encounter can offer to those who are brave enough to share their vulnerability.

Philip went to extreme lengths when he shared with me how incompetent he felt, as a husband, as a person, and ultimately as a therapist. Each of his questions: "Am I able to do any good? Was I a good-enough spouse?" resonates and is amplified in my mind: "Am I? Have I been?" These existential questions do not have a simple, straightforward answer. We all fall short somewhere in some way.

The challenge we all face – no matter our age, gender, culture, social status or the side of the therapeutic screen we are sitting on – is to be able to sit with our own imperfections, accept our past and future shortcomings and keep aiming to become better.

Confer Books are written for all those interested in psychotherapeutic ideas, and designed to deepen our understanding of psychological, relational and emotional processes – to explore concepts that engage with the complexities of being human in an extraordinary era.